Contents

Chapter 15: Other bodies and philosophies evolved from the NHS Plan   76

About the Author

Robert Ghosh

Robert Ghosh is a Consultant Physician at the Homerton University Hospital, London. He is the Director of Intensive Care, Clinical Lead for Acute Care and Trust Lead for Clinical Audit. He graduated from Edinburgh University, and his research interests include the neuromuscular assessment of critically ill patients and prognostication in hypoxic brain injury. He has significant experience in interviewing for Consultant posts; he regularly provides guidance for prospective interviewees, and continues to deliver courses on Consultant Interviews on behalf of Apply2Medicine.

Foreword

If you are reading this book the chances are that you are about to make the most important decision of your professional career i.e. Where shall I work for the next 30 years? Your decision is pivotal in so much that you will spend a significant amount of your lifetime with your colleagues; even more so than your with your partner and family. Your decision must also reflect the investment you have made in yourself over the course of your professional career. The Consultant interview may appear as a mountain, difficult and insurmountable. In reality the mountain is a mole hill and the most difficult question you must ask yourself is 'Is this the correct job for me and do the people around the panel represent the people with whom I wish to spend the next 30 years?'

The Consultant interview does require preparation and as a fully trained professional you will be used to preparing for challenging events. In this book Robert Ghosh presents useful and relevant information to aid you in your approach and emphasises the need for preparation. The role of a Consultant is much wider than the role of Registrar. As a trainee one is often not aware of the full range of duties required of a Consultant. Your preparation must include ensuring that you are educated in all the skills required and aware of the agenda of the National Health Service in general. Preparation for the interview itself requires knowledge of the Trust and of the people involved. The day of the interview looms large but again with preparation the height of the hurdle can be reduced. Think of the likely questions you may be asked and consider your responses using the methods suggested in this book. Only with practice can any skill be developed and honed.

A Consultant is a medical practitioner but also a leader and manager. The professional skills required of a Consultant are continually refined and developed. The interview panel will be aware of the stage you are at in your career and will ask you how you see your career developing. In this book Robert Ghosh has outlined many ways in which this may happen. The panel will not expect you to be an expert in all areas but to have an understanding of the problems faced by modern day Consultants and which areas of your skill base you feel require developing. Having read this book you will need to consider the future development of your career and ensure that you can articulate your learning needs and what contribution your career plan will make to the Trust. Practice those answers, sound like a professional!

Any book is a living entity within a constantly changing world. I trust those of you who read this book and successfully complete the interview process will feed back to us the points that were useful and the points that need to be developed.

Good luck!

Peter Livesley, MMed Sci (ClinEd), MCh Orth, FRCS Orth

Preface

Although the application and interview processes for junior doctors have often been in a state of rapid change, those for Consultant posts have been more predictable and generally remain true to historical values. The post remains exalted in the eyes of medical and non-medical professionals alike. It is therefore paramount that every single potential interviewee gives the interview due respect and sees it as the gateway to the pinnacle of a doctor's career. Preparation should be meticulous.

Although most doctors do invest considerable time, effort and money in academic progression, it is probable that many do not spend the equivalent or sufficient time preparing for that all important Consultant interview. Most interviewees are eligible and skilled doctors who are well regarded by colleagues. They generally have the ability to build excellent relationships with patients. However, these attributes may not be apparent if the performance during the interview is below standard through lack of preparation.

In this book, a few recommendations are dedicated to preparation prior to application, together with some advice on researching and visiting prior to shortlisting. The main remit however, is to help guide you, the prospective interviewee, through the interview process itself. This includes advice with regard to: formal visits; presentations; interview behaviour traits; general principles for answers to commonly asked questions pertaining to factual knowledge, opinion and scenarios.

Interviewers will inevitably take to candidates who possess the capacity for self-reflection, and who can handle clinical and non-clinical stressful situations. Moreover, as many on the Panel will carry some of the Trust's burdens and anxieties, they will have an affinity for candidates who also have a sound working knowledge of Primary Care Trusts, Foundation Trusts, Government targets, complaints, risk, audit, research, education, training, appraisal, job planning, validation, law and ethics. Therefore a great portion of this book contains summaries and questions related to these 'hot topics'.

Some chapters (particularly those relating to technique) are brief; on occasions they are not much more extensive than the summary page! This is a deliberate effort to keep things simple and reassure. The chapters relating to the hot topics are more traditional in size.

Specific detailed advice for academic appointments, for instance Senior Lecturer posts, is not within the remit of this book.

Although this book is not absolutely comprehensive, the information and guidance given here will hopefully go a long way towards equipping the candidate with facts for preparation and insight into behavioural skills. I hope that this will in turn empower you to acquire the confidence to succeed.

Happy reading.

Acknowledgments

I would like to thank my father for teaching me to respect all those around me, Alasdair Short for introducing me to the highest clinical standards, John Coakley for showing me how to relax and most of all, Naomi for giving me perspective.

Matt Green and Apply2Medicine need a medal for their patience and for making it all happen. Sarah Christie, an expert (non-medical) performance coach, has worked very hard to produce the chapter on 'The difference that makes the difference'.

Acronyms and Abbreviations

AHCF	Academic Health Centres of the Future
ARCP	Annual Review of Competence Progression
BMA	British Medical Association
CaB	Choose and Book
CCT	Certificate of Completion of Training
CFH	Connect for Health
CLRN	Comprehensive Local Research Network
CNST	Clinical Negligence Scheme for Trusts
COREC	Central Office for Research Ethics Committees
DoH	Department of Health
ETP	Electronic Transmission of Prescriptions
EWTD	European Working Time Directive
GMC	General Medical Council
HAN	Hospital at Night
HCC	Healthcare Commission
HRG	Healthcare Resource Groups
IBS	Indirectly Bookable Services
IRP	Independent Review Panel
IT	Information Technology
LREC	Local Research Ethics Committees
LSP	Local Service Provider
MCA	Mental Capacity Act
MHRA	Medicines and Healthcare Products Regulatory Agency
MLCF	Medical Leadership Competency Framework

MMC	Modernising Medical Careers
MREC	Multi-centre Research Ethics Committees
NHS	National Health Service
NHS:MEE	NHS Medical Education England
NHSLA	NHS Litigation Authority
NICE	National Institute for Clinical Excellence
NIHR	National Institute for Healthcare Research
NIII	NHS Institute for Innovation and Improvement
NPfIT	National Project for Information Technology
NPSA	National Patient Safety Agency
NRLS	National Reporting and Learning System
NSP	National Service Provider
PACS	Picture Archiving and Communications System
PALS	Patient Advice and Liaison Services
PAS	Patient Administration System
PBR	Payment by Results
PCT	Primary Care Trust
PLAB	Professional and Linguistic Assessment Board
PMETB	Postgraduate Medical Education and Training Board
QMAS	Quality Management Analysis System
RITA	Record of In-Training Assessment
SHA	Strategic Health Authority
SNOMED-CT	Systematised Nomenclature of Medicine Clinical Terms
STA	Specialist Training Authority
SUI	Serious Untoward Incident
UKCRN	UK Clinical Research Networks
WBR	Web Based Referral

Chapter 1 The context and philosophy of the Consultant Interview

Who or what is a Medical Consultant? The On-Line Medical dictionary refers to Medical Consultants as 'Individuals referred to for expert or professional advice or services'. Through the decades, definitions and contexts have changed. The role and duties of Consultants now encompass not only the authoritative and advisory aspect of clinical care, but also increasingly much of the day to day clinical care previously provided by junior doctors. In addition, the management duties previously delegated to other personnel have now come within their remit.

Some individuals may hark back to decades gone by, when the visiting Consultant would sweep into the gravel drive of a private hospital, be greeted by the Matron and taken into her room for tea, prior to conducting a ward round and thereby providing an opinion on the patients in the ward. More recently, salaried NHS Consultants continued to possess attractive work lifestyles; academic activities could easily be provided, job plans were often notional and very flexible, and clinical practice could be adapted to personal whims without financial or managerial recourse.

Most would agree that, in the face of social and NHS modernisation, the job description and work/life balance of the Medical Consultant continue to be very attractive and worth pursuing. Clinical activities continue to be a heady mix of applied science, hands-on intervention, social interaction with patients and colleagues, rapid action, cerebration, academia, camaraderie and authority. The pressures of Government and Trust targets, the need for more availability and concurrent requirement for management skills should all help create a more rounded approach to problem solving, and thereby create better doctors, and indeed better clinicians.

One should approach the commencement of Consultant duties, and therefore the Consultant Interview with excitement and relish. Unmitigated cynicism is a bad starting point, and should perhaps preclude application. This post should be seen as the pinnacle of your career.

There is no doubt that the value and relevance of the Consultant post is given immense respect by all those conducting the interview, and also by other senior personnel in the Trust to which the application is made. This respect, together with the obvious qualities of the job, should prompt the prospective interviewee to make meticulous preparations, and treat the application and interview process with due consideration.

Chapter 1 Key points:

- Absorb the history and know the importance of the job.

- Times have changed: this is not necessarily a bad thing.

- Acknowledge the attributes and wide remit of the job.

- Reflect on the so called 'pressures': know that they generate responsibility, and help develop understanding.

- Approach the job with enthusiasm and respect.

- Be aware that this post is held in the highest regard by all senior personnel within the Trust.

Chapter 2 Preparation prior to Application. Do you feel ready?

Clearly the paperwork (namely the Deanery approval or other pathways to subsequent Specialist Registration, together with the Certificate or definite date for Specialist Registration) must be available at the time of the interview or within the acceptable time frame after the interview. However above all, you the candidate must 'feel ready'.

Your clinical skills should be exemplary, to the extent that you will have repeatedly provided a high quality clinical service without hands on supervision. This characteristic should be assumed as the norm, and will therefore be unlikely to separate the excellent candidates from the good ones in future interviews. The possession of sub-specialty skills may well impact, though they need to be relevant to the needs of the advertising Trust.

Most Consultants agree that it is non clinical skills that separate good from average colleagues. Knowledge of up to date management and political topics is essential. For example, a sound knowledge of the NHS structure and relationships with Acute Trusts, an understanding of the makeup and responsibilities of the Trust Board, and an awareness of recent political issues and proposals will provide a basic framework within which to apply leadership skills. Subsequent chapters in this book will identify topics which you should be aware of, and which are commonly asked in interviews. Leadership qualities are needed daily and in particular at times of stress (to deal with angry colleagues, frustrated patients, resource shortcomings and so on). There is a fine line between authority and arrogance. There are several high quality 'Management courses'; attendance of one of these will usually be mandatory prior to, or just after appointment.

Often, urgent or emergency advice will be sought from Consultants with regard to ethical dilemmas, rather than pure clinical challenges. One should be aware of current opinion. Seeking advice from a colleague is often a better option than procrastination. There is an increasing number of Ethics and Philosophy courses relevant to clinical medicine.

Your career up to this point should have equipped you with significant skills in multitasking and prioritization in the clinical setting. As a Consultant, it is likely that these time management skills will more often be applied to management and other administrative duties. Successful audit, research and administrative activities as a trainee while in the midst of busy jobs should give a good impression.

If you genuinely think that you have ticked these boxes and you 'feel ready', it is time to give the advertisement some serious consideration.

Chapter 2 Key points:

- Possess certificate or definite date for Specialist Registration.

- Clinical skills should be beyond reproach.

- Be aware of management and political topics, and develop leadership skills; if necessary, attend an established course.

- Be aware of ethical issues impacting on clinical decisions.

- Develop time management skills and highlight examples in your CV.

- Above all, you must 'feel ready'.

Chapter 3 Check your credentials and apply

Appointment criteria ('essential' and 'desirable') may be included in the job advertisement, and will certainly be prominently displayed in the job description. Possession of all the essential (and at least some of the desirable) criteria *on first reading of the job description* is an essential starting point. If there is time to acquire an extra criterion prior to application, this is strongly recommended. For example, it is not uncommon for candidates to enroll and attend a worthwhile management course at very short notice. Sadly, many applicants are immediately rejected at the time of application as a result of not meeting the minimal requirements. This reflects badly on the applicant, who clearly has not understood or read the job description, and wastes the valuable time of those involved with shortlisting. A needless rejection will dent morale.

Almost all application forms will be available electronically; the applicant should give time and respect by typing the submission.

The details in the application and Curriculum Vitae should tally. Neither should contain any discrepancies of fact. Common examples include: incongruities of dates and chronology with regard to lists of previous posts; management, research and audit items included in the application though not the CV (or vice versa). Be prepared to be asked about date gaps, particularly if you have not clarified this in your CV. These gaps in years gone by would universally be seen as a negative character-istic. Fortunately, philosophies have changed and it becomes the responsibility of the candidate to identify character-building properties within these periods of time.

There is a fine line between heavily embellishing your CV and frankly lying. Judicious enhancement of facts (usually skills and experiences, particularly in the subjects of teaching, audit and research) is ethical; it is essential however, that this will sit comfortably in your own mind. Be prepared for meticulous dissection during the interview.

Chapter 3 Key points:

- Check your credentials against the appointment criteria: you should possess all the essential criteria, and some or most of the desirable.

- Consider achieving one more criterion at short notice e.g. Management Course.

- Application should be typewritten.

- Include important details in both the application and the CV.

- Check for discrepancies within your application form and CV, and between these documents (e.g. dates in posts).

- By all means prominently display your skills in your CV: do not over-embellish, as you will be exposed in the interview.

Chapter 4 Research the Trust to which you are applying before shortlisting

You will need to ensure that the Trust to which you are applying meets your requirements. Even if you have worked there in the past, there may have been recent changes to affect your working practice. It is important to note how your specialty or specialties are viewed by your potential colleagues, other medical personnel, non-medical staff, managers, the Trust Board, patients and the local Primary Care Trust. Do the personnel in the Department, Directorate and Trust have a reputation (good or bad) for anything in particular?

Much of this information may not be attainable without the time and diligence required from a formal post-shortlisting visit (see Chapter 5). However, informal opinions from junior doctors or other recent employees may be available to you.

All acute Trusts should have established Internet/Intranet sites. Considerable time and effort should be invested in researching the latter. Indeed the quality of the site itself may give you an impression of the quality (or lack) of information and visible priorities of the Trust. Take particular time to investigate the prominence and available information of your relevant Department and Specialty.

Other sources of important information include: the primary care trust website; the Strategic Health Authority website; the Chief Medical Officer's Annual Report (there may be a section in that report which touches upon an issue, or clinical theme, which relates to the post).

If the information gathered so far is satisfactory, you may wish to consider visiting the Trust prior to shortlisting. It would be prudent to telephone or correspond with the Lead Clinician of the Department to establish whether this is acceptable. The aim of this *brief* visit is simply to absorb the atmosphere or 'flavour' of the hospital(s) and department(s), establish the nature of their location and facilities and confirm that you should proceed with your application; arranging formal appointments at this stage is not recommended.

Chapter 4 Key points:

- Is the Trust right for you?

- Do you have any information about how your specialty is seen by others within and outside the Trust?

- Are you aware of any reputations (good or bad) of the Department and/or Trust?

- Visit the Internet/Intranet site.

- Consider other sources of information.

- Consider an informal visit if this acceptable with the Trust.

Chapter 5 Preparation after
shortlisting: the formal visit

Hopefully, selection for interview will instil pride and excitement. Preparations should be made for a formal visit to the Trust, including all its hospital sites. It is true to say that anybody who does not visit the Trust/Department prior to their interview is seriously reducing their chances of success. Organise appointments with the Chief Executive, Medical Director, Clinical Director and Lead Clinician. If you have time, also arrange to see the Directorate General Manager, the Departmental (Modern) Matron and key Executive Directors.

The aim of the visit should be to confirm to some key individuals your reasoning for applying to the Trust, and also to convey to them that you have an interest in the strategic development and anxieties of Trusts. It is useful for key Trust individuals to know, even before the interview, that you take an interest in 'strategy', and that you would like to play a key role in 'development' and problem-solving, if appointed. You may be in a position to factor these issues into the interview.

During the visit, confirm the qualities and features of the Trust which prompted your application. The research described in Chapter 4 will have equipped you for this. It might also be helpful to find out the current research or special interests of relevant panel members, especially if the post is likely to bring you into professional contact with them.

When questions are invited, it would be prudent to enquire

from the Lead Clinician about the department's subspecialty interests. There may be aspects that you were not aware of that are applicable to your skills and expertise. Questions pertaining to clinical shortfalls may be also be directed to the Lead Clinician, though a different perspective to the same question may be provided by the Clinical Director. The Medical Director may have an opinion on perennial managerial problems with regard to the Department and the Trust. The Chief Executive is best placed to discuss the future direction and sensitive topics for the Trust.

When visiting the Department, take time to engage with all the relevant personnel. This may include nursing staff, physiotherapists, technicians and ward clerks.

If you have made time to visit to the Directorate (Operational or 'General') Manager, you may find that (s)he has a unique non-medical perception on the running of the Department or Directorate. This may be important to you, and if it is you may wish to comment during the interview. In addition, the Departmental Modern Matron will be able to give you valuable insight into the issues facing your future nursing colleagues.

It may be relevant to visit key Executive Directors (other than the Chief Executive and Medical Director, who you will have already seen), who will have important opinions on strategic and topical issues. Their roles will include: Corporate Development; Planning; Service Development; Finance; Information; Nursing; Quality; Human Resources; Environment.

In posts which involve split sites one should endeavour to visit all key personnel from all sites. If the sites are within the same Trust, it is likely that the extra visit will involve a satellite department. If the post encompasses more than one Trust, all the appointments mentioned above need to be replicated.

Chapter 5 Key points:

- Organise appointments with the Chief Executive, Medical Director, Clinical Director and Lead Clinician.

- Also consider arranging to see the Directorate General Manager, the Departmental Modern Matron and key Executive Directors.

- Confirm the reasons for your application.

- Lead Clinician: Department's clinical interests.

- Clinical Director: Clinical shortfalls.

- Medical Director: perennial managerial problems with regard to the Department and the Trust.

- Chief Executive: future direction and sensitive topics for the Trust.

- Department: engage with all relevant personnel.

- Directorate General Manager: non-medical perception of the Department or Directorate.

- Departmental Modern Matron: issues for nurses.

- Key Executive Directors: strategic and topical issues.

- You may be able to give these key individuals the impression that you are a problem solver.

- You may be able to factor these issues into the interview.

- Remember, split sites.

Chapter 6 Portfolio preparation, Interview Practice and Dress Code

Portfolio preparation

Most candidates come to the interview equipped with their relevant logbook, if one exists. Most Royal Colleges, Deaneries or Learned Societies have templates or recommended formats available for downloading, and it is essential that this format is preserved, even if it is modified by individuals. Modification and expansion of the logbook to create a comprehensive portfolio is a novel idea, and in my opinion an excellent one. This is best done electronically using spreadsheets, which may be printed out for perusal at the interview. Items dedicated per sheet (in addition to the logbook) may include experiences with: complaints; risk; business cases; difficult clinical situations; situations leading to a change in practice; ethical dilemmas encountered; situations requiring leadership skills; situations requiring management skills; attendance or response to external visits from bodies such as the Healthcare Commission. If questions on these matters are asked during the interview, an articulate response from the candidate may be accompanied by an invitation to the panel to read the relevant item in the portfolio.

Interview practice

The value of interview practice cannot be underestimated. It is recommended that at least two willing Consultant colleagues are identified, though it may initially be useful to run mock interviews with a single interviewer. The venue should be quiet and free from interruptions. It is important that the candidate prepares thoroughly prior to the sessions, which should be taken seriously by both the mock interviewer and mock interviewee. The pre-prepared questions should be asked professionally, and the answers should be delivered in the manner one would expect to see at the actual interview. It may be useful to undergo one final mock interview near the actual day; this would preferably involve two interviewers, with the interviewee having (hopefully) prepared more fully, and perhaps attired formally.

Dress code

Although there is no 'dress code' and the attire is largely a matter of personal choice, one should appear formal, smart and professional and the clothes must feel comfortable. Dark suits are preferable for both men and women. Skirts and trousers are equally acceptable for women. Try to avoid wearing items (such as club ties) which have a chance of provoking tribalism. Ensure your shoes are polished (if appropriate) and clean. Avoid unnecessary strong smells – such as pungent aftershave/perfume, strong cooking odours or cigarette smoke.

Chapter 6 Key points:

Portfolio preparation

- Come equipped with relevant logbook.

- Consider modification and expansion of the logbook to create a comprehensive portfolio.

- Topics may include: complaints; risk; business cases; difficult clinical situations; situations leading to a change in practice; ethical dilemmas encountered; situations requiring leadership skills; situations requiring management skills;

attendance or response to external visits from bodies such as the Healthcare Commission.

Interview practice

- Highly recommended.

- Prepare thoroughly.

- Should be taken seriously by both the mock interviewer and mock interviewee.

Dress Code

- Formal, smart, professional, comfortable.

- Avoid tribalism.

- Avoid pungent aftershave/perfume and spicy food.

Chapter 7 The Interview Panel

It is likely that this will be your first interview where the numbers making up the panel are so large. Each individual panelist will have an important role to play, and their questions will be relevant to their experience and their role.

The Chairman of the Trust will most likely chair the proceeding. He or she is likely to introduce him/herself and the other panelists, and commence the interview process by confirming your identity, and asking some benign questions pertaining to the CV.

The Chief Executive Officer will most often concentrate on concepts of vision, strategy, management, leadership and self-reflection.

The Medical Director may focus on perennial medical problems affecting the Trust. This may or may not have direct relevance to your specialty. Scenario questions may come here or from the Clinical Director/Lead Clinician.

The Clinical Director may have a similar approach to, and type of questions as, the Medical Director. It is more likely that any management or strategy question, for instance Government targets, will have relevance to the Department and Directorate.

The External College Representative is there to provide an external view of previous training, practice development and general competency. He or she may ask you of your perception of any clinical shortfalls in your development or training thus far.

The Lead Clinician is there as a potential close colleague, and will therefore see him/herself as a gatekeeper for the Department. It may be here that your logbook and sub-specialty skills come under the closest scrutiny; visions for progress of the Department may be asked for.

There will be a University Representative if the post is an academic appointment. In addition, more and more District General Hospitals are now University Hospitals, and therefore university representation is required at the interviews. Some questions may be directed at undergraduate teaching. Other complex research politics questions, for instance research funding strategies, research governance, and translational strategies are not within the remit of this book.

The Human Resources representative is unlikely to ask any questions during the body if the interview, and will ask questions on eligibility and commencement-date at the end.

In split site posts there may be duplication of key personnel from the other sites.

Increasingly there are lay people on the panel representing patient and community perspectives. They are there to provide a non-medical stakeholder viewpoint. It is particularly important therefore that your responses to questions are pitched correctly, and that you take into account the varying level of technical understanding of all panel members.

Chapter 7 Key points:

The Interview Panel

- Large panel; each individual has a role
- Chairman
- Chief Executive Officer
- Medical Director
- Clinical Director
- External College Representative
- Lead Clinician
- University Representative (if appropriate)
- Human Resources
- Representatives from other sites in split site posts
- Lay individual.

Chapter 8 The Presentation

It is becoming increasingly common for Trusts to insist on a formal presentation. There are many formats, some being more common than others. It should be appreciated that the formats less frequently employed may become more prevalent in the years to come.

The time of day and duration set aside for the presentation is also not consistent. More often, a half day will be set aside for the candidates to present individually to the panel. Alternatively, the opportunity to present will arise during the interview session itself.

The most common state of affairs is that the topic and audio-visual format will be pre-determined by the Trust, and identified for the candidate significantly in advance. This topic may relate to: your vision for the department/Trust; how you can help the Trust develop; improving clinical effectiveness in your specialty; the future (and controversies) of your specialty; assessing clinical performance in your specialty. When preparing for the presentation, one should consider not only the simple processes involved in achieving the endpoints associated with the topic, but also the relevance of local pressures on the Trust. One may therefore consider: the usage of clinical audit as a tool to improve quality and clinical effectiveness; Trust quality ratings; patient-centered themes.

This is one fictional example:

> *As part of the interview you will be required to provide a 15 minute presentation addressing the following topic: 'Describe ways in which standards are measured in your specialty, and how you can use these to locally maintain clinical excellence'. Please e-mail a maximum of ten slides (A4 – typeset a minimum of 16 using Microsoft Word or PowerPoint) which we will print onto acetates for you to use with an overhead projector (not by PowerPoint projection) as part of your presentation – these slides could include diagrams, key points you would like to get across etc. You will also be expected to answer any questions arising from your presentation – the latter may take up to 15 minutes.*

From the instructions above it is clear that: the presentation must not exceed 15 minutes in length; the slides will be printed onto acetates, therefore you should ensure that your talk flows consistently without the aided technology of PowerPoint; the topic should be clearly stated.

When preparing your presentation it is important that it has an introduction, a main section and a conclusion. When performing a presentation it is important to: introduce yourself and the topic you are going to talk about; provide background or context to the approach you have taken in preparing your presentation; ensure that the main section, and indeed the presentation overall, clearly answers the question or explains your chosen topic.

Some common pitfalls are: not addressing the question or issue that has been requested; talking too quickly; over running on the stipulated time; not speaking loudly or clearly enough; not facing the audience and engaging them; unclear slides; too much information on the slides; using jargon, abbreviations or acronyms; not being equipped to answer questions arising from your presentation.

Less commonly, although the topic is announced in advance, the audio-visual format may not be. This strategy is designed to identify the candidates who will have prepared their thoughts on the subject, and have the ability to modify their delivery. The principles of preparation and pitfalls are similar to those described above.

Rarely, neither the topic nor the audio-visual format is announced until the day of the presentation and interview. For instance, the candidate may be left with an instruction for the topic, together with a flipchart and pens. The purpose of this exercise is to select out the candidate with the ability to *rapidly* identify the reason behind the selection of the topic by the Trust, the salient issues, the possible controversies and also the most efficient method of delivery.

Extremely rarely, behavioural attributes of the candidates may be tested in mock scenarios. The candidates may be assessed individually or in a group. The attributes under consideration may be: ability to deal with frustration; stamina; leadership skills and people management. The history of this type of tactic comes from military recruitment, and more recently from industry.

Chapter 8 Key points:

- Increasingly common; varying formats.

- Half-day set aside, or incorporated into interview.

- Pre-set topic and audio-visual format: look carefully at the instructions; introduction, main, conclusion; consider local pressures on the Trust.

- Pre-set topic, with audio-visual format determined on the day: this needs sound preparation and flexible delivery.

- Topic <u>and</u> audio-visual format determined on the day: this needs *rapid* identification of reason for topic selection and delivery method.

- Be aware of common pitfalls.

- Mock scenarios looking at behavioural attributes: mainly examine the ability to deal with frustration, stamina, leadership skills and people management; this is rare.

Chapter 9 The Difference that Makes the Difference. By Sarah Christie

It's important to acknowledge that *how* you conduct yourself during the interview will be almost as critical to your eventual success or failure as your clinical credentials. You must assume that you are at least on a par with your competitors. 'I am not the preferred candidate' is a commonly quoted grievance. It should therefore be noted that the 'internal' candidate may not be preferred, or may interview very badly. Often there is no preferred candidate at all. One should believe that the interview will be a level playing field. So what are the interviewers looking for?

The period of self-reflection may begin with your recollections of what you have learnt about yourself from previous interviews, particularly if you have received feedback from the panel. Have you addressed the issues raised? Are you now less likely to repeat previous mistakes?

The interview panel will primarily use the interview process to search for a colleague – someone with whom they can work effectively and trust. During the course of forty minutes they will attempt to get to know you and gain an insight into your personality. It is a worthwhile exercise to visualize yourself as a panelist. What would you look for in a candidate? What qualities? What would help you decide the best person for the job? The interview day may be long and arduous for the panel, and it may be difficult for them to recall each candidate. So how are you going to stand out? How are you going to help them decide that you are the person they are looking for?

Set your Outcome

The first thing you must do, well in advance of any interview, is to set your outcome. What impression do you want to create on the day? How do you want them to judge you? Do you want to appear assertive and confident? Competent? Reliable? A team player? A leader? If you haven't given this matter any thought, do so now. It is the first critical step to interview preparation. You must identify the result that you would like, in order to plan for it.

Managing your State

When you look to the future and the interview date, how do you feel? Does the thought of sitting in front of the panel fill you with dread or apprehension? Perhaps the prospect fills you with excitement, knowing that this will be your opportunity to shine. How you represent this event internally at this stage will directly impact upon your behaviour on the day. Begin to explore this now. How do you internally represent 'the interview'? Clearly you need to be in a resourceful state on the big day; if you feel at the moment that there is a lot of ground to cover to achieve that state, this is your chance to act.

Another critical question to ask yourself is this: do you see yourself as a Consultant? Be honest about your feelings. Do you see yourself leading a team? Are you excited at the prospect of managing people as well as attending to your clinical duties? Do you inherently feel like a leader?

It is vital that you answer these questions, as no external individual (in particular, the panelists) will know what beliefs you hold about yourself and your capabilities unless you choose to share them. Your thoughts have a direct impact on how you feel and your frame of mind, which in turn manifest outwardly through your behaviour. If you dread the interview and feel anxious about it, this 'state' will show in your behaviour on the day. If you believe that you are a fraud with little or no credentials to be present at the interview, or if you have determined in advance that you won't be selected, all of these attitudes will influence how you conduct yourself on the day. These unresourceful states will not help you stride into the interview room with confidence.

Outward behaviour is the only characteristic that the individuals on the interview panel have to rely on; they will form a judgment about you, based purely on what they see. It follows, therefore, that you must behave in a way that supports your desired outcome. The only way to do that is to manage your state. Replace negative assumptions with positive ones. If you assume that you are not the preferred candidate, you will undermine yourself. Replace that thought with the assumption that you are *at least* on a par with the other candidates. This attitude should be reinforced by the philosophy that surely you *must* be good enough in order to have been shortlisted.

Are you aware of negative thoughts? Do you say to yourself, 'I hope I don't make a mistake on the day' or 'I hope the Panel doesn't ask me something I can't answer'? If you are aware of this type of negative internal dialogue, make an effort to either switch it off or replace it with positive statements, for example, 'I cannot wait to meet my future colleagues.'

Many people process their thoughts visually and literally 'see' events in their minds. If this is applicable to you, try to examine your inner pictures and movies. Are they supportive of your desired outcome or are they pure horror stories? In the case of the latter, the reassuring reality is that these are your self-created pictures, which are all well within your control and power to change as you see fit. Therefore change the internal movie until you play the ones which support your objective. See yourself doing well at the interview. Imagine the Panel smiling and nodding and shaking your hand as you leave. If these images are realistic, your feelings will respond positively and your state will automatically change. Practise this regularly and you will feel quite differently on the day.

It is unlikely that you will be able to eliminate your nerves completely. However, rather than worrying about this, it would be constructive to use your nerves as a resource. Work with them rather than fight them; allow them to raise your game and give you the edge. Many experts argue that nerves heighten performance on the day.

Using Body Language to Support Your Outcome

It is well known that first impressions count and from the moment you enter the room, the Panel will be assessing you, even if they are doing so sub-consciously. Thankfully, body language is simply a set of behaviours that can easily be shaped to create desired perceptions.

If you want to create an impression of calm, confident, professionalism, enter the room standing tall with your head up, making eye contact with the Panel. Walk with confidence; do not be hesitant. Nod and smile at the Panel if you consider it appropriate. Remember they want to get to know you and a smile of greeting demonstrates your approachability.

When you sit down, make sure that you maintain the body language of assertion and confidence. It's worth sitting in front of a mirror at home, as part of your preparation, to gauge how best to do this. You want to look relaxed and yet professional. Be wary though, that relaxation can easily metamorphose into slouching; the latter is the epitome of sloppiness. Practise some favoured seating positions, and decide which one most supports your desired outcome. For best results, aim for sitting upright with your hands placed comfortably on your lap.

Our hands are the most obvious sign of nerves; pay particular attention to these. Fiddling with rings or necklaces, or even sitting with your hands clasped so tightly the whites of your knuckles can be seen, are all signs of anxiety. Similarly, frantic gestures with hands and arms may be extremely distracting and any of these unconscious habits can alienate the panel.

If you are likely to fiddle with jewellery, consider removing it for the interview. If you curl strands of hair around your finger while you consider the questions being asked of you, consider tying your hair back. Gestures are a useful way of displacing nervous energy, and therefore may have a calming effect, while illustrating a point to the Panel. Although they provide interest it is important that you do not over do them. They should be used in moderation; restrict them for a purpose, perhaps to highlight a point.

Whilst *what* you say is important during the interview, *how* you say it is critical. If you want to convey confidence, the Panel needs to hear that confidence in your voice. Make sure you speak at a moderate pace and that your voice undulates in a way that creates interest. When nerves take over, voices either carry a tremor or sink to a dull, flat, monotone. Practise answering questions with colleagues and get feedback about how your voice sounds. Can they hear your enthusiasm, or passion, or confidence?

It is also critical that you speak with enough volume to convey authority and assertiveness. Do not shout and do not mumble. Consider recording yourself during mock interviews; if you know you are softly spoken, remember to increase your volume for the purposes of the interview.

You are not required to stop being you or change your sense of self. You only need to modify your behaviour – *what* you say and *how* you say it – for the purposes of meeting your outcome on the day. Very small changes can yield amazing results when it comes to creating perceptions.

The Power of Rapport

The single most important thing to do in the interview is to make eye contact with the Panel. This is the most effective way of conveying confidence – being able to look someone in the eye when you talk to them. Nerves may well make you want to look down or away, however this will simply display your discomfort and anxiety. Similarly, do not look up at the ceiling when asked a question. Although this is commonly done when searching for a suitable answer in their mind, it creates the wrong perception. Eye contact is broken, and your rapport with the panel is lost. If you have prepared thoroughly in advance, you should have most of the answers at the forefront of your mind, in order to provide considered answers smoothly and quickly. When answering a question from a member of the Panel, answer that person directly to start with. As you progress with your answer, make eye contact with other members of the Panel too, otherwise they will feel isolated.

Facial expressions too can also help to build rapport. Smile if appropriate and show your sense of humour. Be aware of pulling faces when an awkward question is asked. Unusual or negative facial expressions may encourage the panel to dismiss you as a serious contender.

There is a term called 'mental rehearsing' and this involves you anticipating awkward questions, and practising in your mind how you would answer them. This is quite a separate concept to having a script worked out. Rather, it is the organization of your thoughts and opinions and an approach to answering confidently, with the preservation of spontaneity.

It may be possible for you to shape the answer to a benign question to highlight the qualities you want to demonstrate. Practise answering questions in a manner that guide the Panel into questioning you about topics you are happy to discuss. For example, if you want to convey to the panel that you possess strong leadership qualities, then give examples of where you were able to act as a leader, even if that relates to captaining the local cricket team. Therefore the answer to a question on outside interests will encompass leadership.

The final point relates to the degree of detail or brevity when providing the answer to a question. At times you may feel more comfortable with detail, and launch into your answers with relish. Your eye contact with individuals in the panel however, may reveal that their eyes have glazed over, or they may be looking at their watches. Their body language should be seen as clear indicators that they want you to move on and you may be assessed on whether you take notice, and act accordingly. By contrast, if you give short answers and the Panel wants more, their actions may imply that they want you to expand your answer. Have the flexibility to be able to do so.

When you possess a lot of information relating to the response to a question, be prepared at times not to necessarily share it all at once. Pace your response, and let the panel guide you.

Chapter 9 Key points:

- Know your outcome. Decide on your desired end result and create a plan of how to achieve it.

- You must communicate your personal qualities and you will do so by how you answer the questions.

- Understand that your body language must support your desired outcome. The non-verbal part of your communication must be aligned with your clinical answers.

- The use of voice must also support your outcome.

- Doing your homework and mentally rehearsing the answers to possible questions will greatly reduce your nerves.

- Organise your behaviour on the day so that it does not distract the Panel or lead them to make inaccurate assessments of you. Make it easy for them to focus on your words.

- Remember that the panel needs your help to select you as the best candidate for the job. Make it easy for them!

Chapter 10 Strategies for answers – some general principles

It is not surprising that many questions asked in Consultant interviews centre on topics pertaining to management, leadership and non-clinical attributes. Your future employers and the panel will take your clinical skills for granted, though they will want to be re-assured that your awareness of national management politics, Trust infrastructure and perennial anxieties are sound. The latter may include financial principles, maintenance of standards, external checks for standards, risk, complaints, legal issues and ethical considerations.

It is most important to remember that the interviewers, during the brief 40 minute period, want to get to know you. Are you what they want in a colleague? Well thought-out and articulate answers to difficult questions should give them the impression that you are a good problem-solver, which would be an asset to the Department. One should inwardly dissect the reason behind why the question has been asked; amongst other things, the panel may be seeking evidence of self-reflection, truthfulness or priorities. Once this is clear, it should be a little bit easier to give the interviewers what they want to hear. Identification of the reasoning behind a question will be a recurring theme in this book.

Answers should be brief, relevant, and should wholly answer the question. This may seem obvious; however it is not uncommon to find candidates being either verbose or too brief. The former is more common than the latter.

Most candidates recall successful interviews as a series of conversations, rather than an interrogation. Taking this notion further, the candidate may feel that (s)he is providing valuable, factual information in addition to the required answer, and that this information is being appreciated by the panel. Pleasant, lengthy discussions should not be confused with protracted questioning by the panel in the event of the candidate blatantly not grasping the point of the question!

It is important that the tone of your answers indicate your respect for the panel members and the questions they put to you. However, it is equally important not to sound apologetic. Avoid using phrases such as 'You know' and 'As I previously said' which may be construed to be condescending by the panel.

Always seek to go beyond simply providing a 'textbook' reply. Many candidates do not appreciate that their 'parrot' answers are easily apparent to interviewers. The panel is keen to learn about *you*, rather than simply your skills in recollection.

It is also important to note that any information (for instance expertise in a particular field, such as teaching or research) that is presented in the CV or fashioned into the interview in the form of an answer can become the focus of detailed, in-depth questioning by the interview panel. Therefore it is essential that you do not choose to raise topics that you are not extremely confident about.

Even if you are extremely sure of your ground, the interview is not the forum to express controversial views on a particular subject. You need to strike a balance between demonstrating independent thought and presenting a solid, professional opinion. You need to show that you are an individual personality, yet also someone who can fit into a team and conform to the required standard of conduct.

After completing the introductions, and putting you at ease, the Chairman may begin with some initial questions, which are likely to be introductory and benign in nature. They are not designed to be taxing, and are unlikely to differentiate between interview success and failure. The questions may simply seek to confirm your credentials with the aid of the CV; alternatively, there may be open introductory questions or requests such as 'Why did you apply for this post?' or 'Tell us something about yourself'.

There may be specific questions arising from your presentation. Clearly, preparation and research around the topic should have been performed before the day of presentation, and therefore the questions should not be unpredictable. For the 'ad-hoc' presentations, you should make time to organise your thoughts after the performance, in preparation for questions on the topic or even your method of presentation.

Ensuing questions may be categorized into:

- Those relating to: fact, where an explanation or understanding is sought.
- Those relating to opinion.
- An assessment of the candidate's approach, often by way of a scenario.

Simple questions of fact are relatively uncommon. 'Could you tell me something about the NHS plan?' Here, the interviewer is simply asking for a brief demonstration of your working knowledge. It is more common for there to be some relevance to topical issues or your specialty, and you should take your cue from the interviewer before expanding on this. For instance, a likelier question may be 'Has the NHS Plan delivered for diabetes?'

Questions on opinions are fairly frequent and are traditionally answered badly. 'What is your opinion on junior doctors' training?' The aim here is to demonstrate your identification of 'pros' and 'cons', and then to arrive at a pragmatic and wise conclusion. There is almost never a 'right' or 'wrong' answer. If you choose to firmly commit to a certain view, you should be aware that there will inevitably be individuals on the panel who will disagree, and there is the risk that the whole panel will disapprove of the lack of pragmatism.

In 'approach' and 'scenario' questions, one should rapidly identify the issue or problem. You may wish to demonstrate your methodology with a short introductory explanation, for example 'I believe this is a question of professional/criminal conduct' or 'I believe this is a question of ethics'. In relevant questions you should be aware of processes involved, for example the risk management system, complaints and fitness for practice. One would do well to remember that most roads lead to patient safety and welfare.

Chapter 10 Key points:

- Many questions centre on topics pertaining to management, leadership and non-clinical attributes.

- The panel will take your clinical skills for granted, though they will want to be re-assured that your awareness of national management politics, Trust infrastructure and perennial anxieties are sound.

- Perennial anxieties include financial principles, maintenance of standards, external checks for standards, risk, complaints, legal issues and ethical considerations.

- The interviewers want to get to know you during the interview.

- Articulate answers may suggest good problem-solving skills.

- Answers should not be verbose or too brief.

- Know why a question has been asked.

- Any information that you fashion into the interview in the form of an answer may become the focus of detailed, in-depth questioning from the panel.

- The interview is not the forum to express controversial views.

- Questions pertaining to your presentation: do your preparation; organise your thoughts.

- Simple questions of fact require a brief demonstration of working knowledge – it is common for there to be relevance to topical issues or your specialty.

- Questions on opinions require identification of 'pros' and 'cons', followed by a pragmatic and wise conclusion.

- 'Approach' and 'scenario' questions: identify the issue or problem. Be aware of the processes involved.

Chapter 11 Two vital principles

This chapter is deliberately very brief. The isolation of these principles is intended to highlight their importance, and to give you an opportunity to remember to apply these principles for the questions in the following chapters.

There are often different ways of asking the same question. For example, 'what qualities can you bring to the Trust/ Department?', 'what are your greatest strengths?', 'what do you have to offer us?' and 'why should we recruit you rather than any of the other candidates?' are all asking for differentiating qualities when compared with others. 'Tell us about the two most recent NICE guidelines relating to your specialty. Did you and your department adopt them? Why/why not?' and 'should we always adopt NICE guidelines?' both examine the process of putting evidence into practice. In the ensuing chapters, try to group together the questions which you feel should generate a similar response.

Always attempt to highlight the relevance of your answer to your specialty and the interviewing Trust. For instance very general questions relating to quality or performance, for example the Healthcare Commission, may be seeking an answer dealing with your knowledge of the several roles of the HCC and consequent pressures on Trusts, the specific visits or issues relating to your specialty, your personal involvement with these issues and your ideas on improvement in quality and performance. Other examples include the National Patient

Safety Agency, Strategic Health Authorities and Payment by Results. Be aware that your answer, if of sufficient quality, will give the Panel the impression that you may have the knowledge, insight and solutions to many of the Trust's problems and anxieties.

Chapter 11 Key points:

- Vital: Adopt these principles for the relevant questions in the following chapters.

- There are often different ways of asking the same question. In the ensuing chapters, try to group together the questions which you feel should generate a similar response.

- Particularly in response to questions on quality or performance (e.g. Healthcare Commission, Payment by Results), try to attempt to highlight the relevance of your answer to your specialty and the interviewing Trust, and be aware that your answer, if of sufficient quality, will give the Panel the impression that you may have the knowledge, insight and solutions to many of the Trust's problems and anxieties.

Chapter 12 Questions investigating self-reflection

The interview panel may try to reveal your virtues and weaknesses, perhaps by asking about them directly, or by asking about your aptitudes and ambitions. Answers tend to reveal your personal values. Questions about weaknesses, mistakes, tasks that you could have done better or opportunities missed, set out to measure your self-awareness, intellectual honesty, maturity and dependability; they may also highlight your team membership characteristics.

There are no 'correct' answers to these questions.

Questions about your greatest achievements, challenges or responsibilities are an attempt to obtain a record of your standards. Your challenge may be to identify those which may be more prominent than the average doctor, and indeed more prominent than your competitor candidates. These may include crisis management qualities, negotiation skills or leadership style. Questions about relationships are trying to assess your personality: social or self-contained, conforming or independent; extrovert or sensitive; phlegmatic or excitable.

Questions regarding the post applied for
- Tell us the reasons for applying for this post.
- Why do you want to join our Trust?
- What concerns you about this job?

- What do you think will be your biggest challenge in this post?
- What are you hoping to gain from this post?

These questions are designed to encourage the candidate to reflect on the benefits and drawbacks of the post; this may include issues with the region (poverty, affluence, aged population), the Trust (tertiary services, special attributes), the Department (size, special attributes) or clinical duties (sub-specialty skills at which you are particularly capable). It should be obvious to the Panel that the challenges and drawbacks are not in your eyes insurmountable – after all you have attended the interview! Nevertheless you should articulately clarify your plans to deal with the challenges.

Questions regarding the specialty

- Which attributes of this specialty made you choose it?
- What are the challenges or controversies in your specialty?
- Why did you choose to follow a career in this specialty?
- If you were to start your career again, what would you change?
- Why do you want to pursue this specialty?
- What do you dislike about your chosen specialty?
- How would you dissuade a colleague from entering this specialty?
- What are the challenges facing this specialty over the next ten years?
- What steps have you taken to confirm this is the right career choice for you?
- Can you tell me about what you have done to prepare yourself for a career in this specialty?

The Panel is attempting to obtain a fuller picture of the candidate. The challenges may be national and topical or local (see above). Any dislikes for the specialty the candidate (who has progressed to this level) has, are clearly minor. The 'dissuading' question identifies the candidate who has the ability to recognise the drawbacks of the specialty and correlate this with the profile of the colleague. After performing this exercise you may wish to reassure the Panel that the drawbacks are not relevant to you.

Questions regarding your qualities

- What qualities can you bring to the Trust/Department?
- What is your greatest achievement?
- What are your greatest strengths?
- What do you have to offer us?
- Why should we recruit you rather than any other candidate?
- What makes you a good candidate for the job?
- What three adjectives describe you best?
- What would your friends say about you?
- What are your ambitions as a doctor?
- Where do you see yourself in 2/5/10 years time? What is your ambition as a Consultant?
- What skills have you gained that will make you a good doctor?
- What are the qualities of a good doctor?
- What kind of feedback would I obtain from your patients if I asked them?
- How do you measure success in your field?
- Would you be happy being an average Consultant?

When asked about qualities, achievements and strengths, it would be prudent to remember that many candidates will give stock answers and may simply give an answer 'expected of a Registrar'. You will need to identify strengths that are unlikely to be shared (or spotted) by the other candidates, qualities which would make you an above average senior doctor (for example leadership and management skills) and those abilities particularly relevant to the pressures on the Trust or Department (gleaned from your formal visits).

Questions on self description are intended to highlight self-reflection, and should give the Panel an idea of the type of person you are. Avoid simply singing your own praises.

Remember that ambition may relate to career or personal issues. The former in turn should involve visions for the specialty, the Department and the Trust.

The philosophy of 'being a good doctor' is well encapsulated in the General Medical Council's guidelines which describe the duties of a doctor within the UK:

- Make the care of your patient your first concern.
- Treat every patient politely and considerately.
- Respect patients' dignity and privacy.
- Listen to patients and respect their views.
- Give patients information in a way that they can understand.
- Respect the rights of patients to be fully involved in decisions about their care.
- Keep your professional knowledge and skills up to date.
- Recognise the limits of your professional competence.
- Be honest and trustworthy.

- Respect and protect confidential information.
- Make sure that your personal beliefs do not prejudice your patients' care.
- Act quickly to protect patients from risk if you have good reason to believe that you or a colleague may not be fit to practice.
- Avoid abusing your position as a doctor.
- Work with colleagues in the ways that best serve the patients' interests.
- In all situations you must never discriminate unfairly against your patients and colleagues and must always be prepared to justify your actions to them.

Questions regarding your weaknesses
- What is your greatest weakness?

Every individual has a weakness, and it would be foolish to suggest in an interview that you did not possess one. The Panel is seeking proof of self-reflection, confirmation that the 'weakness' does not impact on patient safety, and that you have taken rectification steps. Commonly volunteered examples of weaknesses include:

'I'm not assertive enough'; 'I often take work home'; 'my time management skills are not ideal'; 'my work/life balance is not great'; 'I do not delegate my responsibilities where maybe I should'. If you have taken obvious rectification steps, for instance the attendance and participation in a time management course, this information should be shared. These examples, though acceptable, serve as examples only. Be aware that if you give a stock response, this will exasperate the Panel; indeed this question is becoming less commonly asked as many interviewers feel that there are already too many stock answers.

Investigating you further

- How do you deal with stress?
- How do you cope with stress?
- What are the major causes of stress to doctors?
- How do you unwind after a hard day's work?
- How do you ensure you maintain your work/life balance?
- What are your hobbies? How do they influence your medical practice?

The working life of a doctor can place enormous stress on individuals which subsequently impacts on their colleagues and families. It is important to demonstrate to the interview panel that you are calm and collected, aware of the potential situations that can lead to stress and be able to manage it appropriately in the acute setting and also with a long term strategy. The panel want to see doctors who lead a balanced working lifestyle.

There are some simple skills and steps that many develop in order to tackle stressful situations:

- Ability to step back and review the situation.
- Identification of the key points causing the stress.
- Being able to share concerns with colleagues.
- Employing more effective time management tools.
- Undertake extracurricular activities.
- Ensure that you have regular holidays with those most important to you.

Other general questions include:

- Describe a difficult case and how you resolved it.
- I see from your CV that . . . Why did you do that?
- What will you do if you do not get this job?
- How do you keep up to date?
- Are you a leader or a follower?
- Do you think all doctors are leaders?
- How many beds are in your Trust? What tertiary services do your Trust provide? Who is your Chief Executive/Medical Director? What is their background?
- What job have you particularly liked/disliked?

The dreaded 'if you do not get this job' question, if asked at the start of the interview, will differentiate between the pessimists and optimists. The former may simply see this question as confirmation that they are not good candidates, and will perform poorly in the rest of the interview. The optimists may simply see this question as a challenge, and will demonstrate dedication to the Panel.

Knowing the makeup and key personnel in the Trust (where you are presently working at the time of the interview) will reassure the Panel that you are an individual with an understanding of the importance of the infrastructure of an institution, and its impact on your working practices.

One may read to keep up to date both clinically and politically. Remember to include learned bodies, websites, journals, academic forums and newspapers. Regular journals or bulletins issued by Trusts may also be helpful in identifying key priorities and issues.

The Consultant post has implicit and explicit needs for leadership. Historically, leadership has been thrust upon and expected from every doctor; unquestioning approaches to doctors' demands reinforced this. Unfortunately, this infrastructure has not lent itself in these modern questioning times, to the development of leadership skills for doctors who now find themselves having to rapidly develop the abilities they were historically expected to have.

The need for development in this field is emphasised in the Tooke report (dealt with later in the book), and further evidence for this is found in the numerous 'leadership' courses for medical staff and the new 'Medical Leadership Competency Framework' (MLCF) from the Academy of Medical Royal Colleges.

The MLCF describes the leadership competencies doctors need in order to become more actively involved in the planning, delivery and transformation of health services. The Framework is a tool which can be used to:

- Inform the design of training curricula and development programmes.
- Highlight individual strengths and development areas through self assessment and structured feedback from colleagues.
- Assist with personal development planning and career progression.

Final approval of the Framework has been received from the Steering Group and Academy of Medical Royal Colleges. They are working with the GMC to integrate the Framework into *Tomorrow's Doctors* and *Good Medical Practice.* The

Postgraduate Medical Education and Training Board (PMETB) will integrate this into College Curricula.

The Framework applies to all medical students and doctors.

It would not be wise, therefore, to volunteer that 'I am always a follower'. However, it is clear that in addition to moments requiring genuine leadership, there are instances where it takes leadership qualities to follow. The latter is not an oxymoron; for example, one may be able to influence others to follow another individual's lead.

'Management' duties may be encountered without too much difficulty during medical studentship and training. These duties may range from:

- Warden duties in halls of residence
- President in Doctors' mess
- On call rota
- Delegated duties for:
  - Risk
  - Complaints
  - Audit.

Chapter 12 Key points:

- These questions aim to measure your self-awareness, standards, intellectual honesty, maturity and dependability.

- Questions about the Post are designed to encourage the candidate to reflect on the benefits and drawbacks of the region, the Department, the clinical duties.

- Questions about the Specialty may involve the identification of national or local challenges.

- Questions on your qualities: avoid stock answers; answers on self description should give the Panel an idea of the type of person you are; ambition may relate to your career (specialty, Department, Trust) or personal issues; remember the principles of being a good doctor.

- Questions on your weaknesses: every individual has one; demonstrate lack of impact on patient safety and rectification steps.

- Questions on stress: demonstrate that you are calm and collected, aware of the potential situations that can lead to stress and be able to manage it appropriately.

- Remind yourself of the ways you keep up to date.

- Re-examine your leadership qualities and be aware of the MLCF.

- Develop and reinforce your management duties.

- Know the infrastructure of your present Trust.

Topics based on key points in history

As mentioned elsewhere in this book, it is unlikely that you will be asked a random question on a key point. This is an interview, not an examination. However a working (not exhaustive) knowledge of key points will allow you to provide coherent answers when asked of their relevance to your specialty.

Chapter 13 Department of Health, and events up to the early 1990s

Figures for reference for the following chapters

The Health structure in England

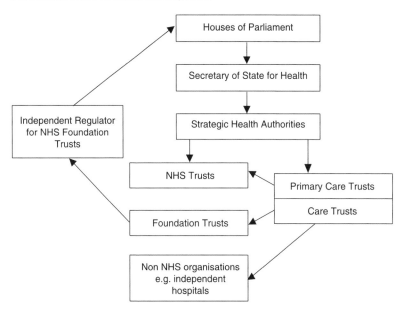

The Health structure in Wales

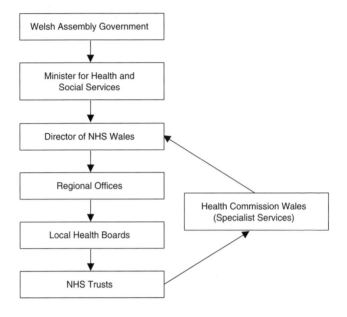

The Health structure in Scotland

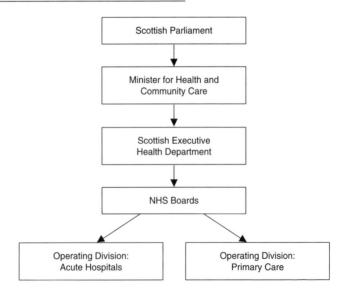

The Health structure in Northern Ireland

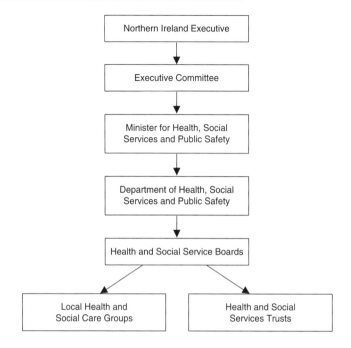

Department of Health

The Department of Health (DoH) is a department of the United Kingdom government, responsible for policy on social care and public health, and is directly responsible for the National Health Service in England. The English system is that which is described in detail in this chapter.

In other parts of the UK, responsibility for health and the management of the NHS has been devolved to local administrations.

• In Wales, the Welsh Assembly, Regional Offices and Local Health Boards oversee healthcare. The Local Health Boards are the budget holders.

- In Scotland, the Scottish Executive Health Department and the NHS Boards wield the power. Clinical advice is given to these bodies by the Area Clinical Forum. Abolishment of NHS Trusts and PCTs occurred in 2004.
- In Northern Ireland, the Northern Ireland Executive and the Health and Social Service Boards provide the central management system. In 2000, the project 'Investing for Health' was initiated; this was comparable in substance to the NHS Plan.

The DoH is led by the Secretary of State for Health (at present Alan Johnson), who is accountable to Parliament. Additional Ministers for Health report to the Health Secretary. At the time of writing, they include: the Minister of State for Health Services (Ben Bradshaw); Minister of State for Public Health (Dawn Primarolo); Parliamentary Undersecretary of State (Professor the Lord Darzi); Parliamentary Undersecretary for Health Services (Ann Keen); Parliamentary Undersecretary of State for Care Services (Ivan Lewis).

Some of the work of the DoH is carried out by 'Arm's length bodies', including Executive Agencies such as NHS Estates, NHS Pensions Agency and the Medicines and Healthcare products Regulatory Agency (MHRA). Like many other UK state departments, the Department of Health has been known by various other names. It started out as the Board of Health, and then became known as the Ministry of Health. It was also for a time combined with social security (the 'Department of Health and Social Security' (DHSS), 1968–1988).

The Department of Health Board is an important body. It supports the Permanent Secretary, who is the Chair of the Board, in the discharge of his responsibilities as the Principal Accounting Officer for the Department. There are three head policy advisors, the lead policy advisor on local government and social care, the head of finance and corporate functions, and three non-executive members who provide external input and challenge. The board is responsible for:

- Advice to ministers on developing the strategy and objectives for the health and social care system.
- Setting DoH standards.
- Establishing the framework of governance, assurance and management of risk.
- Approving the:
  - Departmental Business Plan
  - Resource Accounts
  - Departmental Report
  - Major expenditure commitments as defined in scheme of delegations.

The DoH's Permanent Secretary (at present Hugh Taylor) is answerable to the Secretary of State and Parliament for the way the Department is run. As described above, he chairs the Department of Health Board, and therefore line manages the Social Care, Care Services, Equality and Human Rights, Communications, Corporate Management and Development directorates within the Department.

The NHS Chief Executive (David Nicholson at time of writing) ensures that the Department provides strategic leadership for the NHS and social care.

The Chief Medical Officer (CMO) for England, a key medical advisor to the government, is currently Professor Sir Liam Donaldson (since 1998). He is the UK Government's principal medical adviser and leads key areas of the Department's work.

The other two executive directors are: the Director General

of Social Care, Local Government and Care Partnerships (at present David Behan) and the Director General, Finance and Chief Operating Officer (at present Richard Douglas).

Questions relating to DoH

- What do you think the DoH/Health Secretary/Chief Medical Officer's priorities are with regard to your specialty/this Trust?

As in all factual questions, it is more likely that there will be relevance to topical or specialty-specific issues. As a general rule, the priorities for the DoH will be evident in:

- Medical journals
- Broadsheet newspapers
- Guidelines escalated to SHAs, PCTs and Chief Executives of acute trusts.

The Griffiths Report – the introduction of general management, 1983

In February 1983, the Health Secretary Norman Fowler ordered an inquiry into the effective use of manpower and resources in the NHS. The report was led by Roy Griffiths, Deputy Chairman and Managing Director of Sainsburys in October 1983. He found that there was no coherent system of management at a local level. In addition, there seemed to be no evaluation of its performance against normal business criteria (quality, budgets, productivity, staff motivation, research and development). In June 1984 his recommendations were accepted by Parliament. Subsequently general managers were drawn from inside and outside the NHS in order to be intro-duced into health authorities and into hospitals and units by the end of 1985. Management budgets were introduced into hospitals as was the concept of 'value for money'.

The NHS Training Authority was established and programmes for management training and education were to be increased, particularly for doctors. It was considered essential that senior doctors in particular should be encouraged to be involved in the day-to-day management of the NHS. Various models were tried, though none was successful until the model of the 'Clinical Directorate' attracted support. This suggested that clinical services should be organised into a series of directorates which would each have a Clinical Director or lead consultant, usually chosen by the other doctors within the directorate, to act on their behalf. The Clinical Director was expected to assume responsibility for providing leadership to the directorate and to represent the views of all the clinical specialties. He was expected to initiate change, agree workloads and resource allocation with the unit general manager, and act as the budget holder for the directorate. The relationship between the Clinical Director and colleagues was not seen as one of line management. Rather, the Clinical Director was expected to negotiate and persuade colleagues. Equally, the relationship between the Clinical Director and the unit general manager was seen as one of negotiation and persuasion. The pace at which hospitals introduced clinical directorates varied widely. Eventually the philosophy evolved into the Clinical Director being 'in charge of the doctors' and the general manager remaining responsible for everyone else. The main drawback to implementing the Griffiths Report lay in the simple fact that the NHS had important differences from commercial businesses. There were no major incentives available to persuade those working in the NHS to change their ways of working. Furthermore, for poorly functioning hospitals the traditional commercial sanctions of bankruptcy or takeovers could not apply; the hospital had to continue to offer a service.

Relevant questions

- What can you tell us about the Directorate management structure?
- How does a Directorate improve its management style?
- What does the future hold for doctors in management?

You may be able to demonstrate a working knowledge of the definition and history of the Directorate. In addition to referring to leadership issues (dealt with elsewhere in this book), it may be important to deal with the topics of quality, budgets, staff motivation and clinical governance.

Working for patients, 1989

Heralded as the most formidable programme of reform in the history of the National Health Service in 1989, the DoH developed a White Paper, in which plans were made for the creation of the internal market. These plans were the result of a year long review of Health Services and were designed to make sure that the NHS was a service that put patients first. Efforts were also made to encourage and to organise medical audit within the internal market. Protected funding for this was made available. The two main objectives were to:

- Give patients better health care and greater choice of services.
- Provide greater satisfaction and rewards to NHS staff who successfully respond to local needs and preferences.

The seven key measures were:

- More delegation of responsibility to local level: to make the service more responsive to patients' needs, responsibilities were delegated from Regions to Districts and from Districts to Hospitals.

- Self governing Hospitals: to encourage a better service to patients, Hospitals were able to apply for a new self governing status within the National Health Service as NHS Hospital Trusts.

- New funding arrangements: Hospitals which best met patients' needs were to receive finances to do so; finances required to treat patients were to be able to cross administrative boundaries.

- Additional consultants: to reduce waiting times and improve the quality of service.

- GP Practice Budgets: to help the family Doctor improve services for patients, large GP practices were to be able to apply for their own NHS budgets to obtain a defined range of services direct from Hospitals.

- Reformed management bodies: to improve the effectiveness of NHS management, Regional, District and Family Practitioner management bodies were to be reduced in size and reformed on business lines.

- Better audit arrangements: to ensure that all who deliver patient services make the best use of resources.

Legislation was to be introduced at the earliest opportunity to give effect to those of the above proposals which required it.

The three phases

Phase I, 1989
This was a year of preparation, with the identification of the first Hospitals to be self governing. Regulations were introduced to facilitate easier changing of GP. The first additional Consultant posts were created.

Phase II, 1990

The changes gathered momentum. 'Shadow' boards of the first self governing Hospitals (NHS Hospital Trust) started to develop plans for the future. Medical audit was extended.

Phase III, 1991

The first NHS Hospital Trusts were established. The first GP practice budget holders began buying services. Health Authorities started paying directly for work they did for each other.

Areas of concern at commencement:

- The White Paper concentrated on acute Health Services. There was a lack of Government plans for the development of community based and health provision for people with mental handicap and mental illness. There was no information on preventive health programmes, particularly those concerned with HIV, solvent abuse and alcoholism.

- There were no specific plans for the co-ordination of community care services, for instance, close liaisons between Local Authorities and Health Authorities to ensure effective community care strategies.

- Plans for large General Practices to run their own cash limited budgets, with scope to keep any money left over after they have bought treatment for their patients from Hospitals and Clinics were thought to discourage General Practitioners from taking on the elderly, the chronic sick and people who are disabled.

- Plans were not made for patients treated in Hospitals in another Health Authority's catchment area.

- There was the risk that allowing Hospitals to set their own priorities for any particular speciality they believed would bring in the most money would lead to a lack of incentives to provide expensive services which were seen as less profitable, e.g. the elderly.

Relevant questions:
- Do you believe in the 'internal market'?
- How does the internal market affect your specialty?

The way to deal with 'opinion' questions has been dealt with elsewhere. The advantages and disadvantages should be identified, and a pragmatic approach adopted. It is likely that there will be relevance to your specialty, as the internal market has widespread impact.

Chapter 13 Key points:

- Department of Health: know the basic relevance and history; be aware of new priorities which may have relevance to your specialty.

- Be aware of the history of the introduction of management in the NHS.

- Have a working knowledge of the definition and history of the Directorate.

- Know the history and principles of the internal market, and their relevance to your specialty; be able to refer to topics such as quality, budgets, staff motivation, research and development and audit.

- Do not invest too much time in learning all the historical details. Rather, know the relevance of your specialty and its position with regard to the information above.

Chapter 14 The NHS Plan. Precursors and consequences

The New NHS: Modern, dependable, 1997

The Government set out its vision for the NHS in this White Paper published in December 1997. It described how the internal market would be replaced by a system called 'integrated care', based on partnership and driven by performance. It formed the basis for a ten year programme to renew and improve the NHS through evolutionary change rather than organisational upheaval. These changes were designed to build on what had worked, but discard what had failed. The needs of patients were to be central to the new system.

However by the winter of 1999/2000, hospitals were struggling and the NHS came under sustained attack for its failure to cope with winter pressures, the scarcity of intensive care beds, sub-standard cardiac and cancer care, and its uncaring treatment of elderly people. The Health Services Journal epitomised the NHS as 'under-funded, under pressure and under-appreciated'.

The Prime Minister Tony Blair led the Government's reconsideration of its approach to the NHS. First, in March 2000, came a commitment to a substantial increase in funding for the NHS. Next came a period of work by specialist action teams and of consultation with NHS staff and the public to determine how to use this new money to best effect. The product was *The NHS Plan: A plan for investment, a plan for reform*.

The NHS Plan: A plan for investment, a plan for reform, 2000

Despite its many achievements the NHS was seen to have failed to keep pace with changes in society. The NHS Plan outlined the vision of a health service designed around the patient. There was to be a new delivery system for the NHS together with changes between health and social services, changes for NHS doctors, for nurses, midwives, therapists and other NHS staff. There was also to be a change in the relationship between the NHS and the private sector. The NHS Modernisation Board was set up to advise the Secretary of State for Health and his ministerial team on implementing The NHS Plan.

Ten core principles were established:

- A universal service for all based on clinical need, not ability to pay.
- A comprehensive range of services.
- Services shaped around the needs and preferences of individual patients, their families and carers.
- Responsiveness to the different needs of different populations.
- Continuous effort to improve quality services and minimise errors.
- The NHS to support and value its staff.
- Public funds for healthcare to be devoted solely to NHS patients.
- Working with others to ensure a seamless service for patients.
- Efforts to keep people healthy and reduce health inequalities.
- Respect for patient confidentiality, while providing open access to information about services, treatment and performance.

'Public service agreement' targets were:

- Maximum wait of three months for outpatient appointments and six months for inpatient treatment by end 2005.

- 2/3 of all outpatient appointments and inpatient elective admissions to be pre-booked by 2003/4, and 100 per cent by 2005.

- Guaranteed access to a primary care professional within 24 hours, and to a primary care doctor within 48 hours, by 2004.

- Year-on-year improvements in patient satisfaction.

- To reduce substantially by 2010 the mortality rates from:
    - Heart disease (by at least 40 per cent in people under 75)
    - Cancer (by at least 20 per cent in people under 75)
    - Suicide and undetermined injury (by at least 20 per cent)

- To narrow the socio-economic and geographical health gap (specific targets to be developed in 2001).

- Trusts to meet value for money benchmarks for cost of care.

- NHS in partnership with social services:
    - High quality pre-admission and rehabilitation care for older people; year-on-year reductions in delay in moving people over 75 on from hospital.
    - Increase the participation of problem drug-users in drug treatment programmes by 55 per cent by 2004, and 100 per cent by 2008.

The key financial features were:

- Fixed 1999–2002 three-year settlement over-ridden by March 2000 Budget.

- A commitment to an average annual NHS funding increase of 6.1 per cent UK in real terms over four years 2000–2004.

- Total NHS expenditure in England to rise from £44.5 billion (2000/1) to £56.7 billion (2003/4).

- A step change in capital investment to tackle long-term neglect.

- Flexibility to carry over any unspent planned funding to the next year.

- Increased resources.

Planned investments:

- Over 100 new hospitals between 2000 and 2010.

- 7,000 extra beds in hospitals and intermediate care by 2004.

- 1,700 extra non-residential intermediate care places.

- 20 Diagnostic and Treatment Centres by 2004.

- 500 new one-stop primary care centres, housing GPs, dentists, opticians, health visitors and social workers.

- 250 new scanners, 45 new linear accelerators and other equipment.

- Modern IT in NHS facilities, including patient access to electronic personal medical records and electronic prescribing by 2004.

- Clean wards, better food, bedside televisions and telephones.

- 7,500 more consultants and 2,000 more GPs by 2004.

- 20,000 more nurses and over 6,500 more therapists by 2004.

- Central funding for specialist registrar posts.

- 1,000 more medical school places, in addition to 1,100 already announced, by 2005.

- A new pay system for all NHS staff, and extra pay in shortage areas.
- Childcare support, including 100 subsidised, on-site nurseries by 2004.
- Improvements in occupational health and the working environment.
- £140 million more for staff development, and a Leadership Centre.

Changes to staff:

- All NHS doctors were to participate in annual appraisal and clinical audit; rapid mechanisms for handling under- and poor performance, including a new National Clinical Assessment Authority.
- The majority of GPs were to join the Personal Medical Services scheme by 2004; a revised, quality-based national contract existed for the remainder.
- The option was available for GPs to work on a full-time or part-time salaried basis.
- Hospital care was to be Consultant-delivered. This was dependent on a new Consultant contract, which involved mandatory appraisal, effective job plans and approximately seven fixed sessions per week. There was scope for additional remuneration through accreditation. There was a suggestion that new consultants were to work exclusively for the NHS for 'perhaps' their first seven years; during this time they would provide perhaps eight fixed sessions per week, together with an increased amount of out of hours service.
- New skills and roles were to be given to nurses, midwives and therapists; this would include running clinics, ordering diagnostic tests, prescribing drugs etc.

- 1,000 nurse consultants by 2004, and new consultant therapists.
- 'Modern matrons' with clear authority on the wards.
- Strengthened regulation of the clinical professions.

Changed systems:
- Streamlining occurred at the top of the DoH; a single, more autonomous Chief Executive was responsible for public health functions, the NHS and social services, and reported to a new NHS Modernisation Board on delivery of the NHS Plan.
- 'Earned autonomy' was planned for NHS organisations.
- Core national standards and targets were agreed.
- A Modernisation Agency was developed to support best practice and improvement.
- A mandatory reporting system for adverse healthcare events was devised.
- Independent inspection by the Commission for Health Improvement (CHI) was planned.
- It was agreed that there should be independent publication of performance information.
- £500 million Performance Fund was set up to reward good performance, and intervention was arranged in the case of poor performance.
- Local government was asked to scrutinise the NHS locally.

Inequality targets:
- The Public Service Agreement (PSA) national health inequalities targets were to be scrutinised.
- By 2002 a new health poverty index was to be set up to

combine data about health status, access to health services, uptake of preventive services, and opportunities to maintain health.

- Reducing inequalities was to be a key criterion for NHS resource allocation by 2003.
- Action to reduce inequalities was to be assessed through the NHS Performance Framework.
- New formulae and incentives were designed to improve the distribution of primary care staff; Medical Practices Committee was abolished.
- New screening programmes were to be instituted.
- Free fruit was to be made available for young school children.

Patient convenience:

- NHS Direct was to become a one-stop gateway to out-of-hours healthcare by 2004.
- Better out-of-hours pharmacy services were to be developed, more over the counter medicines, repeat prescriptions from the pharmacist, and delivery of medicines to the patient's door.
- More tests and treatment in primary care (as opposed to hospital consultants) and up to 1,000 new specialist GPs.
- On the spot booking systems were to be created for hospital appointments.
- NHS Direct nurses were to check on older people living alone.
- Free translation and interpretation was to be provided in all NHS premises via NHS Direct.

Older people:

- A National Care Standards Commission was to be set up in 2002 to drive up standards in domiciliary and residential care.

- A National Service Framework on services for older people was to commence.

- Resuscitation policies would be a requirement in all NHS organisations.

- A pilot was to start in 2001 of a free NHS retirement health check.

- Breast screening would be provided for women aged 65–70.

- Personal care plans would exist for all.

- There would be a new 'Care Direct' service, more home care and support, as well as more intermediate care.

- Subject to Parliament, there would be free nursing care in nursing homes.

- But not free personal care.

Patient information and empowerment:

- A Patient Advocacy and Liaison Service (PALS) was to exist in every Trust by 2002.

- There would be a reform of procedures for complaints and 'informed consent'.

- A new NHS Charter would be developed by 2001.

- The abolition of Community Health Councils would occur, in favour of a Patients' Forum in every Trust and a local advisory forum in every Health Authority.

- There would be patient and/or citizen representation on the NHS Modernisation Board, each Trust Board, CHI teams.

- A new Independent Reconfiguration Panel was to advise on contested major service changes.
- A new Citizens' Council would advise NICE on clinical assessment.

Performance targets:

- The NHS Plan (2000) proposed that NHS organisations should be performance-assessed against government targets and priorities (set out in the Plan) and given ratings.
- These ratings were published by the Department of Health for the first time in September 2001, in respect of acute hospital Trusts only (based on their performance in 2000–1).
- All acute Trusts in England were rated on their performance against Key targets (using the rating options for each target of Achieved, Underachieved and Significantly under-achieved). They were also rated (using a five-point scale) on the following focus areas:
  - Clinical focus
  - Patient focus
  - Capacity and capability
- Trusts were assessed using a 'Balanced Scorecard' method (intended to allow for the relative strengths and weaknesses of each individual organisation) to produce an overall composite assessment from zero to three stars.
- In July 2002 acute Trusts received their second annual ratings (relating to performance in 2001–2), alongside the first performance ratings for specialist hospital Trusts and ambulance Trusts (using the same system as for acute Trusts). The performance of Primary Care Organisations was assessed for the first time against a range of suitable indicators, but they were not given an overall star rating.

CHI: Commission for Health Improvement (CHI) 1997

In December 1997, the idea for a commission for health improvement (CHI) was mooted in New Labour's first health policy white paper, The New NHS. It proposed an arms length statutory body to 'monitor, assure and improve' clinical systems in NHS providers, with powers to intervene in failing trusts. In June 1998, yet another white paper, 'A First Class Service – Quality in the NHS', was published outlining further details of how CHI would work, including its role as a 'troubleshooter'. By June 1999, the Health Act 1999 received royal assent and CHI was created. Operations began in April 2000, and publications of the first routine clinical governance reviews were completed in December 2000.

Another landmark was August 2001, when Epsom and St Helier hospitals NHS trust was the subject of CHI's critical routine inspection report. It uncovered high death rates, 20-hour trolley waits, filthy toilets and patient complaints that took too long to resolve. The Trust Chief Executive became the first manager to resign directly as a result of a CHI report. In November 2001 the NHS reform bill was published. This followed the recommendations of the July 2001 public inquiry into children's heart surgery at Bristol Royal Infirmary. The bill proposed new powers for an NHS inspectorate, including the ability to suspend services at failing trusts, to inspect private health facilities where NHS work was carried out and to publish an annual state-of-the-NHS report. In response to this the then chancellor, Gordon Brown, made a budget speech in April 2002, outlining a five-year 43 per cent increase in NHS funding. He unveiled plans for a new super-inspectorate to keep track of NHS performance. Subsequently the NHS Reform Act 2002 expanded the powers of CHI to include performance assessment of the NHS. This indicated that CHI would publish NHS star ratings in future. The performance ratings published by CHI in July 2003 (relating to 2002–3) covered all acute, specialist, ambulance and mental health Trusts – and all Primary Care Trusts (PCTs).

Subsequently, CHI was merged with the Mental Health Act Commission, the National Care Standards Commission and parts of the Audit Commission to form the Commission for Healthcare Audit and Inspection (CHAI), which was operational from April 2004. (A new Commission for Social Care Inspection for England was also created at the same time.) It was subsequently decided that CHAI would be known as the Healthcare Commission (HCC).

Healthcare Commission, 2004

The Healthcare Commission (HCC) was established under the Health and Social Care (Community Health and Standards) Act 2003 and is known in legislation by its full name, the Commission for Healthcare Audit and Inspection. The Commission came into being on 1 April 2004 and has the general function of encouraging improvement in the provision of health care by and for NHS bodies in England and Wales. The Commission's functions include:

- The work previously undertaken by CHI; the latter ceased to exist in March 2004.
- The private and voluntary healthcare work of the National Care Standards Commission (NCSC); this also ceased to exist in March 2004. The NCSC was an independent body established by the Care Standards Act 2000, responsible for regulating independent sector care services, including healthcare services, in England.

- The work of the Audit Commission, relating to value for money in healthcare. The Audit Commission is an independent organisation that promotes the best use of public money by local authorities and other bodies – it has additional powers under best value legislation.

The HCC powers therefore cover two distinct though complementary roles – audit and inspection. The Commission was also given a range of new functions including handling the second stage of the NHS complaints process and the coordination of reviews into healthcare. The Commission published its new Annual Health Check in October 2006 that provided in-depth performance measurements of NHS trusts.

The HCC published the ratings for 2003–4 in July 2004; and those for 2004–5 in July 2005 – this was the last usage of the star system. Since then, a different rating system has been used, with Annual Performance Ratings for each Trust being generated through the Annual Health Check, which is carried out by the HCC. In the AHC, the first Annual Performance Ratings (covering 2005–6) were issued in October 2006 and the second (covering 2006–7) in October 2007. The third set (covering 2007–8) at time of writing is due to be published in October 2008. Under the Annual Health Check, all NHS Trusts in England were given an Annual Performance Rating on two counts: quality of services and use of resources. The scales ranged from 'excellent' to 'weak' (via 'good' and 'fair').

The Use of Resources score was derived from work done by each Trust's auditors and the Audit Commission (which compiled an Auditors' Local Evaluation score for each Trust) – or Monitor, in the case of Foundation Trusts.

The Quality of Services score was an aggregation of each

Trust's scores when assessed against the following benchmarks, set by the government:

1) Core Standards. In respect of each individual core standard, Trusts were rated using the options 'compliant', 'insufficient assurance' or 'not met'. This lead to an overall rating of 'fully met', 'almost met', 'partly met' or 'not met'.
2) Existing National Targets (using the rating options 'fully met', 'almost met', 'partly met' or 'not met')
3) New National Targets (using the rating options 'excellent', 'good', 'fair' or 'weak'.

If an organisation scored 'not met' for either Core Standards or Existing National Targets, it was automatically given a score of 'weak' for Quality of Services. This was the only way that an organisation could receive a score of 'weak' for Quality of Services. Different rules applied to mental health Trusts.

Overall Quality of Services scores are still not directly comparable across different organisation types (PCTs, acute Trusts, Ambulance Trusts, etc.). This is a result of the differing number of Existing Targets and New National Targets that apply to each type. Direct comparisons of overall Quality of Services scores are thus only valid within an individual organisation type (i.e. when comparing PCTs with PCTs, acute Trusts with acute Trusts, etc.).

In each Annual Health Check, Trusts are required to assess themselves and submit declarations on how far they have achieved each Core Standard, using sets of criteria issued by the HCC. As part of the declaration process, Trusts are responsible for seeking commentaries on their performance against Core Standards from 'third parties'. These may be Strategic Health Authorities, Patient and Public Involvement Forums

(Local Involvement Networks from 2008–9), Local authority Health Overview and Scrutiny Committees or Elected Governors (in the case of Foundation Trusts). Third parties are not expected to sign off, or comment directly on, Trusts' declarations. Rather, the Trusts must include third-party commentaries, word-for-word, with their declarations to the HCC. In turn, the third-party commentaries are cross-checked by the HCC against Trusts' declarations. Depending on the information received from third parties, the HCC may investigate a Trust further, by means of a risk-based inspection (to which around ten per cent of Trusts are subjected each year).

The Commission also carries out random inspections for the purpose of quality assurance (involving a further ten per cent of Trusts each year). According to its findings, the Commission can deduct penalty points, and adjust Trusts' declarations, where appropriate.

The government intends to create a single regulatory body for health and social care by merging the HCC with the Commission for Social Care Inspection and the Mental Health Act Commission, to form the Care Quality Commission (CQC – it has also been referred to as 'Ofcare'). The legislation to enact this measure, the Health and Social Care Bill, at time of writing is before Parliament. It is intended that the new Commission will be established in October 2008, taking responsibility for the regulation of health and adult social care in April 2009 and working towards the full implementation of a new registration system from April 2010. The existing Commissions will continue to fulfil their functions until the end of March 2009 to allow for an adequate transition period to the new arrangements.

This means that responsibility for finalising and publishing the results of the Annual Health Check for 2008–9 will rest with the CQC. There will be significant changes to the Annual Health Check for 2008–9, including the following:

- All acute Trusts will be inspected to check on compliance with the Hygiene Code.
- PCTs will be assessed on their performance as commissioners of services, separately from their performance as service providers.
- Assessment against National Priorities will replace the measurement of performance against Existing National Targets and New National Targets.

One should be aware of the high profile national targets set by the government year-upon-year. Many or all of these will have some bearing on your specialty.

Relevant questions:

- Where have we got to, with regard to the NHS Plan and your specialty?
- Has the NHS Plan delivered for your specialty?
- What exposure have you had to the Heath Care Commission?
- How are standards measured for your specialty/the Trust?
- Are you aware of the interfaces your specialty has with the Health Care Commission?
- In what ways do you think your specialty can maintain/ improve this Trust's standards, as measured by external bodies?
- What processes could you help put in place to set standards for your specialty?
- What do you think is the most significant government target with regard to your specialty?

The Healthcare Commission and the maintenance of Government standards are topics which form the basis for many sleepless nights for Chief Executives and Medical Directors! Status for excellence (and indeed Foundation status) will depend on the success or failure in achieving these standards. It is understandable, therefore, that these issues will be revisited time and time again in various Trust forums. It follows that a solid understanding of the relevance of Government standards to your specialty, and ideas for pursuing these standards, will play a fundamental role in the outcome of the interview. After dealing with Government standards, one must not forget to mention the standards pertaining to quality and academia.

Chapter 14 Key points:

- White Paper: The New NHS: modern, dependable.

- The NHS Plan: A plan for investment, a plan for reform, 2000: core principles, public service agreement' targets, key financial features, planned investments, changes to staff, changed systems, inequality targets, patient convenience, older people, patient information and empowerment, performance targets.

- CHI

- Healthcare Commission

- Do not invest too much time in learning all the historical details. Rather, know the relevance of your specialty and its position with regard to the NHS plan, and your specialty's interface with the Healthcare Commission, standards and targets.

Chapter 15 Other bodies and philosophies evolved from the NHS Plan

Adverse healthcare events and risk

An expert report on risk in the NHS ('An organisation with a memory') was conducted by the Department of Health in 2000, led by the Chief Medical Officer. It was found that the adverse incidents, though uncommon, had devastating consequences. The consequences were costly, and there was a familiar ring to most of the errors. The problems at the outset were:

- Often the picture was incomplete.
- 400 people died or were seriously injured in adverse events involving medical devices.
- Nearly 10,000 people were reported to have experienced serious adverse reactions to drugs.
- Around 1,150 people with recent contact with mental health services committed suicide.
- Nearly 28,000 written complaints were made about aspects of clinical treatment in hospitals.
- The NHS paid out around £400 million a year settlement of clinical negligence claims.
- There was an estimated liability of around £2.4 billion for existing and expected claims.
- Hospital acquired infections – around 15 per cent of which may have been avoidable – were estimated to have cost the NHS nearly £1 billion.

• NHS was not good at learning lessons: when things went wrong an individual or individuals were identified to carry the blame. The focus of incident analysis had tended to be on the events immediately surrounding an adverse event, and in particular on the human acts or omissions immediately preceding the event itself.

The proposed way forward:

• Unified mechanisms were recommended for reporting, and analysis when things go wrong.

• A more open culture.

• Mechanisms for ensuring that the necessary changes were put into practice.

• A much wider appreciation of the value of the system approach in preventing, analysing and learning from errors.

In the following year (2001) a further report ('Adverse healthcare events: Building a Safer NHS for Patients') was issued by the Department of Health. The Government accepted all the recommendations in 'An organisation with a memory', and also accepted that successful implementation depended on:

• The commitment of all NHS staff and the boards of all NHS organisations and Trusts.

• The creation of a culture where staff feel that they can report errors, mistakes and adverse events without fear of retribution.

• The establishment of clear national and local mechanisms for reporting mistakes and near misses and analysing trends.

• The learning of lessons to reduce risk and prevent future harm to patient.

Outcomes from the reports described above:

- The National Patient Safety Agency (NPSA), established in July 2001, co-ordinates efforts to identify and learn from mistakes. Health workers are encouraged to report incidents that they have witnessed without fear of reprimand. The NPSA is looking at how the public could report to it directly using the internet or a confidential hotline.

- Clinical Negligence Scheme for Trusts had already existed since 1994. It was a means by which Trusts funded costs of litigation and provided effective management of claims. It is administered by the NHS Litigation Authority (NHSLA).

- The National Reporting and Learning System (NRLS) draws together reports of patient safety incidents and systems failures from health professionals across England and Wales. It helps the NHS to understand the underlying causes of problems and act quickly to introduce practical change.

- An integrated approach to investigating errors across the NHS and different agencies.

- The following authorities developed relationships to the bodies above:

  - The National Clinical Assessment Authority (a special health authority set up to provide a support service to health authorities and hospital and community trusts faced with concerns over the performance of an individual doctor. It is now part of the NPSA as 'National Clinical Assessment Service, NCAS').
  - The General Medical Council.
  - The Healthcare Commission.

Questions which may be asked:

- Have you had any dealings with your Trust's Risk Department? How does it work?

- How many types of meetings have you attended recently, which have dealt with clinical risk?

- Can you recall being involved in a clinical situation which involved clinical risk? How was it dealt with?

- How is risk dealt with in your present department or directorate?

- Have you ever filled in a 'Serious untoward incident ('SUI') form? Whose hands did it go through? What actions did you take to follow up?

- Has your department any strong interfaces with the NPSA/NRLS?

It is probable, if one took time to reflect, that most days in clinical practice involve decisions about, or assessment of, clinical risk. It would be ideal that most directorates and departments in the NHS had specific meetings for risk, in which all doctors regularly attended. Sadly, this is not the case at present. It is important, therefore, that doctors, particularly senior trainees, identify risk meetings relevant to their specialty, and make a point of regularly attending. All Trusts and all directorates have registers of clinical and non clinical risk. There should be evidence of consistent handling and cross-directorate learning.

It is vital that any 'adverse incident' forms are followed through. A thorough understanding is essential of: the type of personnel in the department responsible for risk; their responsibilities in dealing with adverse incidents; the process of actions; method of recommendations. It is good practice for the individuals responsible for submission of the adverse incident form to check the status of assessment. Conversely, the risk department should as a matter of course feed back to these individuals.

The NHS Modernisation Agency

This was established in April 2001. It was designed to support the NHS and its partner organisations in the task of modernising services and improving experiences and outcomes for patients. There have so far been four areas for focus: improving access, increasing local support, raising standards of care, and sharing knowledge.

NHS Direct

This is a 24 hour, confidential telephone, online and interactive digital TV health advice and information service provided by the National Health Service in England and Wales. The organisation has been given Special Health Authority status. It was rolled out between 1998 and 2000, and a similar service was introduced in Scotland in 2004 (where it is called NHS24). The telephone service aims to triage callers to provide guidance on which healthcare provider the caller should access. Nurses also give advice on how to manage an episode of illness at home. In some areas of the UK, NHS Direct is commissioned by local Primary Care Trusts to provide the gateway for out-of-hours access to GP's surgeries and clinics, and also to emergency and routine NHS dentistry. The website contains a self-help guide and also a comprehensive health encyclopaedia. There is also an online enquiry service, which is similar to the telephone-based health information service, where visitors to the site can request information via e-mail.

National Service Frameworks

These are long term strategies for improving specific areas of care, such as UK's largest causes of morbidity and mortality, other common conditions and key patient groups. They set national standards, identify key interventions and put in place agreed time scales for implementation. These aims are achieved by being inclusive – developed in partnership with health professionals, patients, carers, health service managers, voluntary agencies and other experts. The topics at present are:

- Hypertension
- Cancer
- Mental health
- Children
- Chronic obstructive pulmonary disease (COPD)
- Coronary artery disease
- Diabetes
- Long term conditions (neurological and other)
- Stroke
- Vascular disease
- Renal disease.

Two main roles include:

- The setting of clear quality requirements for care based on the best available evidence of what treatments and services work most effectively for patients.
- The offering of strategies and support to help organisations achieve these.

Questions which may be asked:

- What examples of NSF standards can you give me for your specialty?
- How would you maintain these standards?

These questions investigate the same issues as those dealing with standards relating to the Healthcare Commission.

Patient Advocacy and Liaison Service (PALS)

The NHS Plan set out to establish a new system of patient and public involvement (PPI) to replace Community Health Councils in England as part of the modernisation programme. The system was also designed to respond to the Bristol Royal Inquiry report, which recommended representation of patient interests 'on the inside' of the NHS and at every level. PALS, which is available in all Trusts, are a central part of PPI in England and provides:

- Confidential advice and support to patients, families and their carers.
- Information on the NHS and health related matters.
- Confidential assistance in resolving problems and concerns quickly.
- Information on and explanations of NHS complaints procedures and how to get in touch with someone who can help.
- Information on how you can get more involved in your own healthcare and the NHS locally.
- A focal point for feedback from patients to inform service developments.
- An early warning system for NHS Trusts, Primary Care Trusts and Patient and Public Involvement Forums by moni-

toring trends and gaps in services and reporting these to the trust management for action.

- Liaisons with staff, managers and, where appropriate, other relevant organisations, to negotiate speedy solutions and to help bring about changes to the way that services are delivered.

- Referrals for patients and families to local or national-based support agencies, as appropriate.

Questions which may be asked:

- Have you had any dealings with PALS?

- Have you ever witnessed a complaint from a patient or a relative about you, your colleagues or your department? What was the outcome?

- Are you aware of what 'PALS' do (other than deal with complaints)?

Data

The Data Protection Act in 1984 dictated that clinical data should be relevant, accurate, updated, processed formally, not for disclosure, kept only as long as necessary, accessible and correctable by the patient and secure. These days, there are named custodian(s) designated to ensure confidentiality, and there are strict terms of internet usage (the searches, browsing and software need to be in context). Security and storage should be applied using passwords.

National Project for Information Technology (NPfIT)

This initiative to move towards electronic care records for patients was formally established in 2002. Subsequently in 2005 a new Department of Health agency 'NHS Connecting for health' was formed to deliver the programme. The aim is also to connect GPs to acute Trusts, and ensure the access is secure and auditable. Eventually patients may also have access to their records. In Wales a similar programme is running ('Informing Healthcare').

The programme is divided into a number of key deliverables. These are:

- The NHS Care Records Service (NHS CRS).
- Choose and Book, an electronic booking service (see below).
- A system for the Electronic Transmission of Prescriptions (ETP).
- A new national broadband IT network for the NHS (N3).
- Picture Archiving and Communications Systems (PACS).
- IT supporting GPs including the Quality Management and Analysis System (QMAS) and a system for GP to GP record transfer.
- Contact – a central e-mail and directory service for the NHS.

There are plans to create a 'core data' storage and messaging system, known as the 'Spine', which will:

- Store personal characteristics of patients, such as demographic information.
- Store summarised clinical information which may be important for the patient's future treatment and care.
- Provide the security systems required to restrict access to the national and local systems.
- Provide a secondary users service, using anonymised data to provide business reports and statistics for research, planning and public health delivery.
- Bind together all the local IT systems within the programme.

The programme divides England into five areas known as 'clusters': Southern, London, Eastern, North West and West Midlands, and North East. For each cluster, a different Local Service Provider (LSP) is contracted to be responsible for delivering services at a local level. This strategy was intended to avoid the risk of committing to one supplier which might not then deliver.

In addition to these LSPs the programme has appointed National Service Providers (NSPs) who are responsible for services that are common to all users e.g. Choose and Book and the national elements of the NHS Care Records Service that support the summary patient record and ensure patient confidentiality and information security. There have been several changes to service providers.

NPfIT has been criticised for inadequate attention to security and patient privacy. For example the consent arrangements for creating and adding information to the Spine have not been well communicated to patients or clinicians. In particular, debate has arisen over whether an 'opt-out' or 'opt-in' system should be used. In fact, a hybrid consent system is now proposed: an 'opt-out' system will be used for the creation of the Spine, while the addition of clinical information will happen on an 'opt-in' basis. More will be done to explain these arrangements, particularly to patients.

Important components of the Spine have not yet been completed. 'Sealed envelopes' will allow patients to restrict access to particularly sensitive information and are an important safeguard for patient privacy. Advocates of the system note that these concerns must be set alongside the necessity of care professionals having access to personal medical data if they are to deliver safe, high quality care. The balance between the right to privacy and the right to the best quality care is a sensitive one. There are sanctions against those who access data inappropriately – specifically instant dismissal and loss of professional registration.

Worryingly, in a January 2005 survey among doctors, support for the initiative as an 'important NHS priority' dropped to 41 per cent, from 70 per cent the previous year. There had been concerns raised by clinicians that clinician engagement has not been addressed as much as might be expected for such a large project. However supporters of the scheme suggested that the only other choice was to do nothing and this was unacceptable.

The project was originally expected to cost £2.3 billion over three years. However more recent Government estimates put the cost of the programme at between 20 and 30 billion pounds, although it is expected that this will be recovered in 'savings and other benefits'.

Connecting for Health has set out to replace local IT systems across the NHS, and build the capacity to link these systems together. The new national broadband network has now been completed, but progress in other areas has been disappointing. In particular, the introduction of new basic hospital Patient Administration Systems (PAS) has been seriously delayed. As a result of these and other delays, it is not clear when joined-up systems will be widely available. Connecting for Health will publish clear, updated plans, indicating whether and how the project has changed since 2003.

An important cause of the delays has been the lack of local involvement in delivering the project. As a result, they have lacked the incentives or enthusiasm to take charge of deployments. Increasing local ownership is now a key priority for the programme.

Safe and effective data sharing also requires a more standardised approach to the recording of clinical information. To this end, the agreement on a universal coding language for the NHS, SNOMED-CT, and a single unique patient identifier, the NHS number, are important achievements. Also, in the future, the HealthSpace website will allow patients to access their data from home and has great potential for making care more patient-centred.

NPfIT has no links to the equivalent system in Wales and there is no similar system yet proposed for Scotland. This is in keeping with the continuing trend of devolution of government reponsibilities. Nor are there immediate plans to include opticians or dentists.

Choose and Book (CaB)

This is an application which has been introduced from 2005 onwards, to enable patients needing an outpatient appointment to choose which hospital they are referred to by their general practitioner, and to book a convenient date and time for their appointment. It was procured as part of the NPfIT in 2003. Surgery where immediate treatment is required is not in the remit of Choose and Book. Such patients' needs bypass any longer-term queuing systems. In its fully functional mode, Choose and Book communicates electronically between 'compliant' GP Clinical Computer systems and Hospital Patient Administration Systems (PAS). For a number of reasons a number of GP and PAS Systems have not been made compliant in time to deliver the Choose and Book targets set by the Department of Health. Interim solutions were devised to allow patients to benefit from CaB during 2005/6.

Web Based Referral (WBR) allows a GP to access Choose and Book via a standard Web Browser until their Clinical Computing system can be successfully upgraded.

Indirectly Bookable Services (IBS) involves telephone Call Handlers in Hospitals to offer CaB appointments to patients.

The commencement of CaB in 2005 suffered some delays: some technical (as a result of its dependency on other NPfIT work streams), some functional (problems in early releases), and some through clinicians' concerns about additional workload. However, since the application became more stable during 2005, volumes have increased steadily. By early July 2006, over 500,000 patients in 3,500 GP Practices have benefited from CaB. Where it is being used most patients report an improved service and like it. However, there have been detractors who have been put off by the idea of booking online. Some patients have complained that the system is too confusing. In addition, it is still possible to book through CaB without entering some important clinical data, and there are anecdotal reports that much relevant information pertaining to the nature of the referral/booking is lost when viewed at the provider end. For example, it has been documented on occasions that doctors seeing CaB patients in the Outpatient Department do not have any information other than the name of the patients and demographics.

Joint Guidance on Protecting Electronic Patient Information

This is a joint piece of work by British Medical Association and NHS Connecting for Health. The philosophy is that everyone in the NHS has a responsibility to understand the implications of dealing with electronic patient data, and provides key guidance to facilitate awareness of responsibilities. The NHS Code of Confidentiality deals with:

- Computer log-out
- Security of logins and passwords
- Data visibility on screen.

Organisational responsibilities include:

- Security, information governance and records management policies must be in place.
- This should be endorsed by the Board or senior partners and updated at regular intervals.
- Organisations must complete:
  - Information Governance Toolkit which measures progress against a series of standards.
  - Information governance statement of compliance, which ensures that organisations that use NHS CFH services meet certain standards.
  - Part of the toolkit includes a section on the transfer of batched patient data.
  - The default position is there should be no transfers of unencrypted person identifiable data held in electronic format across the NHS.

Staff responsibilities include:

- Awareness of good practice with regard to security.
- Possession of regular training including:
  - What information they are using.
  - How it should be used.
  - How it should be handled, stored and transferred.
  - What procedures, standards and protocols exist for

the sharing of information with relevant others and on a 'need to know' basis.

– How to report a suspected or actual breach of information security within the organisation, to an affected external information service provider or to a partner organisation.

NHS Connecting for Health responsibilities include:

• The construction of 'smartcards' (to enable log-ins).

• The definition of 'legitimate relationships', that is grouping of users for relevant data.

• The clarification of 'role-based access'; different degrees of data are accessible to different users.

• The facilitation of audit trails and alerts; this will allow tracking of usage.

Questions which may be asked:

• Do you have electronic patient records where you work?

• What are the benefits and drawbacks?

• How could information technology impact better with your specialty?

• What are the controversies these days in information technology?

• Are you in favour of 'Choose and Book'? Does Choose and Book work?

NICE

The National Institute for Health and Clinical Excellence (NICE) is a Special Health Authority of the National Health Service. It commenced as the 'National Institute for Clinical Excellence' in 1999, and in April 2005 amalgamated with the

Health Development Agency to become the 'National Institute for Health and Clinical Excellence' (still abbreviated as NICE). It was originally established to review clinical approaches, and also help defuse the so-called 'postcode lottery' system of healthcare, where the application of some effective therapies at times seemingly depended upon where patients happened to live. NICE publishes appraisals of particular treatments, and provides recommendations upon their effectiveness, and cost-effectiveness. NICE assessments must take into account both desired medical outcomes and also economic arguments regarding differing treatments.

Since 2005, the NHS in England and Wales has been legally obliged to provide funding for medicines and treatments recommended by NICE. The appraisal of an intervention or technology by NICE goes through discrete stages:

- The intervention or technology must have been referred to NICE by the Secretary of State for Health.

- The ensuing appraisal stage includes patient groups, organisations representing health care professionals and the manufacturers of the product undergoing appraisal. Also, additional organisations are included, such as manufacturers of products to which the product undergoing appraisal is being compared.

- An independent academic centre then draws together and analyses all of the published information on the technology under appraisal and prepares an assessment report.

- Comments are then taken into account and changes made to the assessment report to produce an evaluation report.

- An independent Appraisal Committee then looks at the evaluation report, and hears spoken testimony from clinical experts, patient groups and carers. They take their testimony into account and draw up a document known as the appraisal consultation document.

- This is sent to all consultees and commentators who are then able to make further comments.
- Once these comments have been taken into account the final document is drawn up. This is called the final appraisal determination.
- This is submitted to NICE for approval.

Questions you may be asked:
- What is the role of NICE?
- Tell us about the two most recent NICE guidelines relating to your specialty. Did you and your department adopt them? Why/why not?
- Should we always adopt NICE guidelines?

It should be understood that NICE is but one credible source, sometimes in a selection of many. On occasions, guidelines from different credible sources may conflict. It is up to professionals to demonstrate that guidelines pertaining to their specialty have been discussed in appropriate forums, and the reasoning for adopting certain policies is documented. On occasions, there may be a requirement from the DoH to describe whether a certain NICE guideline has been adopted. In these situations, the reasons for not adopting should be logged with the department (clinical governance issue) and the relevant Trust body (for instance the Clinical Effectiveness/ Clinical Audit Committee).

Commissioning a Patient-led NHS
In July 2005 the then NHS Chief Executive Nigel Crisp announced a process to 'create a step change in the way

services are commissioned by front line staff, to reflect patient choices'. The paper stated that the changes were necessary because 'improvements in commissioning, the determination to make progress on working with Local Authorities on Choosing Health, and the commitment to make £250 million of savings in overhead costs, require NHS organisations to change and develop'. The main changes envisaged were a restructuring of Primary Care Trust (PCT) and Strategic Health Authority boundaries, placing an emphasis upon the commissioning of health services.

The direction of travel is now clear: Primary Care Trusts will become patient-led and commissioning-led organisations with their role in provision reduced to a minimum.

The reconfigured, restructured Primary Care Trusts and Strategic Health Authorities came into being in 2006.

Questions which may be asked:
• How does the 'patient-led NHS' affect your specialty?
• Do you think that the 'patient-led NHS' is a good thing?

Acute Trusts
Acute Trusts run hospitals (see the recent chapter on the 'NHS Plan'). Unless they are Foundation Trusts, they are accountable to the Strategic Health Authority. There are, in addition, Mental Health Trusts, Ambulance Trusts and Children's Trusts (which include health, education, social services).

Foundation Trusts
NHS Foundation Trusts (often referred to as 'Foundation Hospitals') are hospitals which are non-profit making, are part of the NHS and have a similar relationship with PCTs to non-Foundation Trusts. Nevertheless they have a significant

amount of managerial and financial freedom which non-Foundation Trusts do not have. The introduction of NHS Foundation Trusts represented a profound change in the history of the NHS and the way in which hospital services were managed and provided. The philosophy centres on 'ownership' by the local community and therefore a 'patient-led' NHS. This is achieved (or attempted to be achieved) by more significant representation of the community on the Board of Governors. The original purpose was to devolve decision-making from a centralised NHS to local communities; the cynics saw the change towards semi-independent hospital boards as a move towards privatisation of the health service.

A key difference for foundation trusts is that they are not accountable to the local Strategic Health Authority, but rather directly to the Department of Health through the Independent Regulator ('Monitor'). Technically, they are not even under the directorship of the Secretary of State. The first ten such Trusts were approved in April 2004.

Advantages of Foundation Trusts are:
- Faster decision making in financial matters are possible.
- There is more flexibility in financial matters (e.g. borrowing).
- There is more opportunity to plan ahead strategically.
- In theory, there is greater community influence in the running of the Trust by way of the community representation in the Board of Governors.

Disadvantages/limitations of Foundation Trusts are:
- A restriction is placed on the number of private patients which can be treated.
- If there is a conflict in philosophies in service provision between the Board of Governors/community and the PCT,

the wishes of the PCT still carries greater influence (as a result of contractual obligations) than the wishes of the Board of Governors.

Questions which may be asked (if you are applying to, or coming from, a Foundation Trust):

• What are the advantages or disadvantages of Foundation Trusts?

• Would our status as Foundation Trust make us more or less attractive to you?

• How could your specialty help us succeed in becoming a Foundation Trust?

Yet again, this last question is related to standards and Health-care Commission pressures, as successful applications for Foundation status are based on sound financial plans and clinical standards.

Primary Care Trusts

All primary care services are managed local Primary Care Trusts (PCTs). They exist to service local NHS needs and to ensure satisfactory numbers and quality of General Practitioners. In addition to these management responsibilities, Primary Care Trusts also commission the provision of the care provided by NHS Hospital Trusts.

Also, PCTs work with Local Authorities and other agencies that provide health and social care locally to make sure that local community's needs are being met. Primary Care Trusts are now at the centre of the NHS and receive 75 per cent of the NHS budget. As they are local organisations, they are in the best position to understand the needs of their community, so they can make sure that the organisations providing health and social care services are working effectively.

Individual/Group Practices may hold and manage an indicative budget for health care. This is called 'practice-based commissioning'. The savings are used to improve local services (with PCT approval). Legally the PCTs still hold the budgets (and the risks) and are responsible for delivery of targets.

The 'lead PCT' hosts and manages the allocated budget for the SHA area. It also handles disputes between constituent PCTs, and provides expertise on local procurement issues. It may lead on the prioritisation of investment proposals. At times the lead PCT may be a virtual arrangement, rather than a physical one.

The Department of Health calculates a 'target allocation' for every PCT based on four Key Factors:

• Numbers
• Need
• Distance from Target
• Pace of Change.

Questions which may be asked:

• How do you think PCTs see your specialty?
• How do you think partnerships between acute Trusts and PCTs could be developed in your specialty? If we were to appoint you, how could you develop our relationship/partnership with the PCT?

There is a drive for acute Trusts to work more in partnership with PCTs. This is a consequence of the 'patient led NHS' and the Darzi report (see elsewhere in this book). There may in addition, be finances available for relevant treatment directly in the gift of the PCT, whereas the Trust may have more pressing financial pressures. Although informal 'networking' occurs between Consultants and GPs, ideas for innovations for working in partnership with PCTs should be formally examined by the Trust Board. Ideas from Consultants, therefore, should be discussed with the Chief Executive, who may then organise meetings within the Trust to facilitate liaisons with the PCT.

Strategic Health Authorities

These were created by the Government in 2002 to manage the local NHS on behalf of the Secretary of State. In particular, they were to ensure robust Lead PCT arrangements were in place, and that investments in capital schemes reflected national and local strategic priorities. There were originally 28. In July 2006, this number was reduced to ten. Fewer, more strategic organisations were thought to be able to oversee stronger commissioning functions, leading to improved services for patients and better value for money for the taxpayer. Strategic Health Authorities are responsible for:

- Developing plans for improving health services in their local area.
- Making sure local health services are of a high quality and are performing well.
- Increasing the capacity of local health services – so they can provide more services.
- Making sure national priorities – for example, programmes for improving cancer services – are integrated into local health service plans.

All Primary Care Trusts and NHS Hospital Trusts (other than Foundation Trusts) are accountable to Strategic Health Authorities.

Other bodies given 'Special Health Authority' status

This is given to the following:

- National Patient Safety Agency (NPSA – described earlier in this chapter).

- The National Institute for Health and Clinical Excellence (NICE – also described earlier in this chapter).

- National Clinical Assessment Authority (referred to with regard to 'changes to staff' in the NHS Plan in Chapter 13 and also with regard to adverse healthcare events earlier in this chapter).

- National Blood Authority. This is an integral part of the NHS. It manages the National Blood Service, and therefore guarantees to deliver blood, blood components, blood products and tissues from 15 blood centres to anywhere in England and North Wales. It also ensures that the supplied blood (which is dependent entirely from voluntary donations) is properly screened and is safe for patients. Other functions include interfaces with research, the provision of specialist medical advice and clinical support to hospitals, and educating and training transfusion medicine specialists.

- NHS Information Authority. This is a special health authority that provides facts and figures to help the NHS and social services run effectively. It collects data from across the sector, analyses it, and then converts it into useful information. It was previously known as the National Case Mix Office. The recent priorities have been:

  - Patterns of prescribing and compliance with NICE guidelines.
  - Supporting the patient choice agenda
  - To integrate NHS and independent sector information

(support and guidance will be extended to private sector providers)
- Using financial data more effectively
- Widening the use of Electronic Staff Record (ESR) data
- Improving and developing better social care information
- Supporting SHAs with their information needs to answer policy issues
- Promoting clinicians' use of information.

Payment by results, and some other particulars with regard to finance

The PCTs receive 75 per cent of the NHS budget. (The remainder of the monies are distributed to bodies and institutions, including arms length bodies). For services which cannot be provided directly by the PCT, 'service level agreements' (SLAs) are arranged with providers; these arrangements deal with quantity and quality of provision, and are legally binding.

Historically, hospitals were paid according to 'block contracts' – a fixed sum of money for a broadly specified service – or 'cost and volume' contracts which attempted to specify in more detail the activity and payment. But there was no incentive for providers to increase throughput, since they received no additional funding.

Subsequently the Government, through the NHS Plan, signaled its intention to link the allocation of funds to hospitals to the activity they undertook. It stated that in order to get the best from extra resources there would need to be some differentiation between incentives for routine surgery and those for emergency admissions. Hospitals would be paid for the elective activity they undertook. This in theory offered the right incentives to reward good performance, to support sustainable reductions in waiting times for patients and to make the best use of available capacity. The aim of Payment by Results (PbR) would be to provide a transparent, rules-based system for paying trusts. It would reward efficiency, support patient choice and diversity and encourage activity for sustainable waiting time reductions. Payment would be linked to activity and adjusted for casemix. Importantly, this system would ensure a fair and consistent basis for hospital funding rather than being reliant principally on historic budgets and the negotiating skills of individual managers. Competition between providers would also be encouraged by this system.

The Department of Health consulted on its plans for introducing PbR in 'NHS Financial Reforms: Introducing Payment by Results' on 15 October 2002 and published its response on 10 February 2003.

Presently, the agreed price of a service may be based on the average cost of the service across all providers in England ('national tariff'). This is applicable to most elective and acute services and includes: outpatient new attendances; outpatient follow-ups; outpatient procedures; elective and non-elective admissions; A&E attendances. At the time of writing, the national tariff does not cover primary care, community care, mental health and ambulance services. By 2008 or 2009, Home Births will be included in the national tariff. If there is no national tariff, the local price ('local tariff') is paid. The cost of health care varies across the country, just as salaries, land and house prices vary. The Department of Health therefore, calculate the 'Market Forces Factor' to reflect this variance and apply it to both PCT allocations and the national tariff.

Early implementers and Foundation Trusts are at the time of writing already using PbR for elective work. The Government aim is for PbR to account for 90 per cent of all hospital activity by 2008/2009.

Healthcare Resource Groups

The Casemix Service develops and supports Healthcare Resource Groups (HRGs), which are standard groupings of clinically similar treatments which use common levels of healthcare resource. The prime purpose of HRGs is to assist the Department of Health to implement the policy of Payment by Results. They also:

- Offer organisations the ability to understand their activity in terms of the types of patients they care for and the treatments they undertake. The activities which may be referred to include:
  - Clinical governance
  - Performance monitoring
  - Caseload management/review
  - Programme-based resource analysis and allocation
  - Costing and commissioning (this is accepted as the main priority).
- Enable the comparison of activity within and between different organisations and provide an opportunity to benchmark treatments and services to support trend analysis over time.

HRGs are used as a means of determining fair and equitable reimbursement for care services rendered. These consistent 'units of currency' support standardised healthcare commissioning across the service. The current version of HRGs (v3.5) has been in use since October 2003.

The Casemix Service has completed a major revision, HRG4. This has been in use for reference costing from April 2007 (for financial year 2006/07 onwards). It is a major revision that introduces HRGs to new clincial areas, to support the Department of Health's policy of Payment by Results.

Questions you may be asked:

- How relevant is PbR to your specialty?
- Do you agree with PbR?
- What are HRGs? What aspects of care in your specialty do you think HRGs will focus on?
- Can you describe any problems that need resolving with regard to HRG/PbR and your specialty?
- How could you help this Trust engage your Consultant colleagues and other doctors in producing high quality and timely discharge summaries in your specialty?

Satisfactory correlation between identification of the complexity of the outpatient/inpatient, the acute and chronic diagnoses in the inpatient, the interventions and the outcome (morbidity/mortality and discharge date) relies on satisfactory coding. Recognition of (and payment for) the activities of the Trust in turn relies on the timely delivery of the coded documentation (usually a discharge summary). In virtually all specialties, the outcome prediction, the clinical performance rating and tariff will be dependent on the entry of any complex co-morbidities for a given intervention (e.g. surgery or treatment of pneumonia). Omission of complexities in the acute and chronic diagnoses, and those of interventions and treatments, therefore may lead to an optimistic outcome prediction, diminished performance rating and diminished tariff. Trusts should therefore deploy systems which ensure satisfactory coded descriptions of patients, and timely discharge summaries. This will always involve doctors and coders working in partnership with other staff. An age old problem which has not been satisfactorily resolved in all Trusts is 'how does the Trust engage Consultants and other doctors in producing high quality and timely discharge summaries?' The answer lies in the acceptance of the discharge summary (and its associated mandatory items i.e. diagnoses, interventions and HRG/PbR correlations) as a non-negotiable product, and to make its production mandatory within a given time frame.

Although HRGs should not be seen as the omnipotent bible for quality references in clinical work, one may as a matter of course regularly refer to relevant HRG material while striving for clinical excellence in one's specialty.

Chapter 15 Key points:

- Adverse healthcare events and risk

- The NHS Modernisation Agency

- NHS Direct

- National Service Frameworks

- Patient Advocacy and Liaison Service (PALS)

- Electronic data

- NICE

- Commissioning a Patient-led NHS

- Foundation Trusts

- Primary Care Trusts

- Strategic Health Authorities

- 'Special Health Authorities'

- PbR and HRG

- Remember: intricate facts are not important, though facts relevant to your specialty are!

Topics relating to professional bodies and concepts

Basic (not exhaustive) knowledge, and relevance to your specialty is important!

Chapter 16 Bodies responsible for validation and appraisal

It should be remembered that the concepts of validation, appraisal and service provision are often blurred and confused. Validation is a process which protects *the patient*. Appraisal protects the quality of training or career development of *the doctor*. The job planning process *ensures service provision for the Trust*, although it simultaneously provides a vehicle for career development and therefore appraisal.

Validation bodies

A. The General Medical Council (GMC)

The GMC was formed in 1858, and is the regulator of the medical profession in the United Kingdom. Its main purpose is to protect, promote and maintain the health and safety of the community by ensuring proper standards in the practice of medicine. It provides the licence for doctors to enable them to practice, and has the power to revoke this licence, or place restrictions on a doctor's fitness to practice. A practitioner not registered with the GMC is forbidden to present themselves as a registered medical practitioner in the UK.

The GMC also contributes to regulation in medical schools in the UK, and liaises with other nations' medical and university regulatory bodies and their medical schools overseas. This leads to some qualifications being mutually recognised. The

Council is funded by annual fees required from those wishing to remain registered and fees for examinations.

A registered medical professional may be referred to the GMC if there are doubts about his or her fitness to practice. These are divided into concerns about health and other concerns about ability or behaviour. Hearings may result in reprimands, restrictions on practice temporary suspension or erasure from the register. The processes adopted by the GMC need to have substantial agreement in principle from government and from many medical bodies (e.g. the BMA, the Royal Colleges). Over the years, the development of public confidence has been a priority.

The GMC also administers the Professional and Linguistic Assessment Board test (PLAB), which has to be taken by non-European Union overseas doctors before they may practice medicine in the UK.

The main guidance that the GMC provides for doctors is called 'Good Medical Practice'. This summarises the standards and behaviours that are expected of them, and the document is at present subject to a lengthy consultation process.

Three types of GMC licence exist:

- Provisional – Provisional registration is granted to those who have completed medical school.
- Limited – Limited registration is granted to foreign graduates who have completed the PLAB examination but require a period of work in the UK before their registration can be converted to 'full'. This mode of registration is expected to be discontinued.
- Full – Provisional status may be converted into full

registration upon satisfactory completion of the first year of postgraduate training.

Since 2001, the GMC has itself become answerable to the Council for Healthcare Regulatory Excellence (CHRE), which is a UK health regulatory body set up under the 'National Health Service Reform and Health Care Professions Act' of 2002. The CHRE is an independent public body, funded by the Department of Health and answerable to Parliament. It was set up to co-ordinate standards and good practice amongst the bodies responsible for regulating the healthcare professions in the UK, in the wake of the Kennedy Report into paediatric cardiac surgical services at the Bristol Royal Infirmary. It commenced its work in April 2003. The CHRE may overturn previous GMC verdicts.

Subsequently, the government White Paper, 'Trust, Assurance and Safety – The Regulation of Health Professionals in the 21st Century', published in February 2007, set out a series of proposals for further reform of medical regulation. The reforms proposed were welcomed by the GMC, who believe that they will lead to an improved and robust system of regulation.

At the time of writing, Secretary of State for Health had announced that the Postgraduate Medical Education and Training Board (PMETB, see later) will be merged with the GMC in the near future. The decision followed a recommendation made by Professor Sir John Tooke in 'Aspiring to Excellence: Final report of the Independent Inquiry into Modernising Medical Careers' (see later in this book). The merger will bring under one roof the regulation of all stages of medical education; this in turn may deliver benefits for patients and the public, as well as for the medical profession.

At present, a doctor may annually self-re-validate, simply by not being involved in any ongoing fitness to practice GMC issues, and by paying the annual fee. However, in future, revalidation will have three outcomes:

- Registration without the privileges of relicensing.
- Relicensing, with the accompanying legal privileges of being a doctor (including prescribing and completing death certificates); it is likely that this process will occur cyclically, for instance every three or five years, and will be linked to a meticulous local appraisal procedure (in addition to 'standard' annual appraisal events).
- Recertification for those on the Specialist and GP Register; the process for this is unclear at the time of writing.

B. The Postgraduate Medical Education and Training Board (PMETB)

The PMETB is an independent statutory body, responsible for overseeing and promoting the development of postgraduate medical education and training for all medical specialties, including general practice, across the UK. It assumed its statutory powers on 30th September 2005 taking over the responsibilities of the Specialist Training Authority of the Medical Royal Colleges (STA) and the Joint Committee on Postgraduate Training for General Practice (JCPTGP). The PMETB's responsibilities include establishing, promoting, developing and maintaining standards and requirements for postgraduate medical education and training across the UK.

The PMETB is primarily responsible for:

- Establishing national standards and requirements for postgraduate medical education and training.
- Making sure these standards and requirements are met by monitoring.

- Developing and promoting postgraduate medical education.
- Awarding Certificates of Completion of Training (CCT) and determine eligibility of doctors for inclusion on the Specialist and GP Registers.

The PMETB is currently funded by grants from the Departments of Health in England, Northern Ireland, Scotland and Wales. These will decline in value until 2009/10 when the PMETB will seek to be self-funding. Income will be generated through various initiatives which may include increased fees for CCT and applications under Articles 11 and 14.

Unlike the Specialist Training Authority (STA), PMETB is independent of the Royal Colleges. The STA is a body of the Royal Colleges whereas the PMETB is a statutory competent authority established by Parliament. However, the PMETB works closely with the Royal Medical Colleges by way of liaisons with their commissioning services.

Therefore it is clear that PMETB has dual roles in both validation and appraisal.

Appraisal processes

A. Record of In-Training Assessment (RITA)
The purpose of a RITA is to record the annual review of trainee progress through training programmes towards CCST/CCT. Its main functions are to:

- Ensure the trainees have had appraisals and feedback from their educational supervisors.
- Review the accuracy of the proposed CCST date.
- Check the completeness of the logbook/training record.

- Plan the next year of training.
- Provide career advice.
- Review the quality of training posts.
- Review the duty rota.

The panel members are:
- Postgraduate Dean (or representative).
- Training Programme Director /STC Chair.
- Regional advisor or specialty advisor.
- External assessor.
- University trainer (for clinical academic trainees).

The following questions are usually asked of the trainee:
- Has the previous year been useful from a training perspective?
- What were the good/bad points?
- Were there adequate opportunities to increase skills?
- Was there adequate supervision?
- Was there sufficient time for private study?
- Were necessary facilities readily available?

The following points may be addressed by the panel:

- What competencies are still required?
- How and where is this to be arranged?
- How will the trainee's needs be accommodated in conjunction with those of other trainees?
- Are there any particular problems that need to be addressed?

There is usually scope for confidential feedback, and there is a vehicle for appeal if the trainee is not satisfied with the process.

The RITA will gradually be replaced by an updated process, termed the Annual Review of Competence Progression (ARCP).

B. Annual Review of Competence Progression (ARCP)

This is replacing the RITA process, and is also therefore an important process in gaining accreditation. It was conceived as an updated formalised assessment of a trainee's progress towards the achievement of a CCT (Certificate of Completion of Training). It has to be a transparent process, capable of standing up to public scrutiny. To achieve this, senior colleagues within each specialty have defined criteria, based upon the relevant curricula. At the time of the ARCP meeting, the progress of the trainee is set against this set of pre-defined criteria. In turn, this will be recorded regionally and at the Royal College to which the trainee will ultimately be recommended as a doctor who has reached a standard compatible with independent practice.

C. Appraisal systems for Consultants

The term 'appraisal' should not be confused with 'validation' or 'performance management'. While the general public is protected by validation (see 'GMC' above), and the employer receives value by way of performance management, appraisals should be seen solely as vehicles to protect the practice development for the Consultant (and training for the trainee – see 'RITA' and 'ARCP'). This is an opportunity for the Consultant to meet with a peer to set objectives and improve the quality of career development.

Appraisals may occur at any frequency, and they may be formal or informal. The minimum requirement is for Consultants to be appraised annually and formally. The appraiser therefore needs to be an individual with knowledge of the concept of practice development, and a basic understanding of the requirements for development. It need not therefore be a Clinical Director, Lead Clinician or a colleague from within the same specialty as the appraisee. Indeed, it may be preferable for the appraiser not to be linked to Trust management, to avoid confusing the issue of practice development with those of service provision for the Trust.

Behavioural issues interfacing with validation, appraisal and service provision

Clearly, there may be instances where an issue (such as rudeness to patients) may simultaneously impact on practice development, validation and performance for the Trust. In these cases, the appraiser should make the relevant recommendations for improved practice, and subsequently inform the appraisee that separate forums may be required to deal with the issues of validation and Trust performance. After careful consideration, a decision would be made with regard to reporting to the GMC. The Trust would also take a view in relation to disciplinary processes. It should be noted that, during disciplinary hearings in the Trust, the doctor in question will be entitled to legal and union representation. Therefore, the term 'disciplinary' should always be used reservedly.

Topics included in Consultant appraisals include:

- Medical care
- Medical practice
- Relationship with colleagues

- Relationship with patients
- Teaching and training
- Probity
- Health
- Research
- Management
- Clinical audit
- Appraisals may be linked to job planning, in order to tailor the job plan to the needs of the Consultant.

Questions which may be asked:

- What is the difference between appraisal and validation?

- If we were to appoint you, who would you expect to appraise you, and how often? What particular topics do you think you ought to be appraised on?

- Do you think the present system for validation for doctors is satisfactory? Do you agree with the proposed changes?

- Do you think that the current Consultant appraisal process is satisfactory? Is it just a 'tick box' interview? How do you think we can improve the quality of appraisals for Consultants?

In response to the last 'tick box' question, it may be worthwhile considering the formalisation of CPDs, and clinical audit projects, with appraisal sign-off only occurring with evidence of the latter.

Chapter 16 Key points:

- Examples of, and differences in the meaning of, appraisal and validation

- GMC, PMETB

- RITA, ARCP

- Proposed changes in validation for doctors

- Appraisal process for Consultants

- Methods for improvement of the Consultant appraisal process

- Intricate facts are not important, though facts relevant to your specialty are!

Chapter 17 Other important bodies and concepts

The British Medical Association (BMA)

The BMA is the professional body to which the vast majority of British doctors belong, and owns the British Medical Journal, one of the world's more prestigious medical journals. It dates from approximately 1860, when it was established by the amalgamation of several regional medical associations. It allows doctors to be represented both by the geographical area in which they work, and by the various craft committees. The craft committees comprise (in alphabetical order):

- Central Consultants and Specialists Committee
- General Practice Committee
- Junior Doctors Committee
- Medical Academic Staff Committee
- Medical Ethics Committee
- Medical Students Committee
- Public Health Medicine and Community Health Committees.
- Staff and Associate Specialists Committee.

The BMA has sole negotiating rights for national Terms and Conditions of Service for doctors working in the National Health Service. It also supports public health initiatives (such as a ban on smoking in public places), responds on behalf of doctors to consultations by Government, and promoting the views and reputation of doctors in different arenas.

The Colleges and Royal Colleges

The relevant (Royal) College will often issue information and opinions on current affairs, training and topics pertaining to your specialty. The interview panel will include a representative from the relevant Royal College (although this is not mandatory for Foundation Trust interviews). It is therefore important that one keeps up to date with the latest matters and developments.

The College representative may deal with questions regarding:

- Modernising Medical Careers and European Working Time Directive (see below).
- Training issues in general.
- Controversies and political issues pertaining to your specialty.

Modernising Medical Careers (MMC)

This was implemented by the government in August 2005 with the aim of providing a more consistent, structured, efficient and shorter training programme for junior doctors. The aim was that MMC would help to facilitate the introduction of the European Working Time Directive (EWTD) into the working hours of junior doctors, by making the training more relevant and efficient. The shortening of the time taken to reach consultant level will in theory help address the shortage of consultants within the NHS, though some cynics feel that the quality of training is compromised. The old format of postgraduate training for junior doctors is gradually being replaced, and trainees of the new program will also undergo more regular and structured assessments of the skills they have learnt to ensure they are of the required standards. It is envisaged that these assessments will be conducted by a variety of professionals including consultants, senior nursing staff and communication experts.

The format comprises of:

- Foundation Year 1: This is equivalent to the old style Pre-Registration House Officer year. The curriculum is based on the GMC's guidelines for 'Good Medical Practice' and the primary aim of this year is to promote this practice.
- Foundation Year 2: This is equivalent to the old style first year of SHO training. In this year the curriculum addresses the doctor's competency in coping with a variety of emergency situations.
- Core Training: This will replace the senior SHO/early SpR years. The length of this will differ depending on speciality but will normally be two years in duration and will provide an introduction to the chosen specialty.
- Higher Specialist Training: This will replace the latter stages of the old style SpR training. The duration will differ depending on the speciality but normally be three years in duration and provide a more in depth training into the selected specialty.

The introduction of MMC has caused great controversy and debate as to whether it will actually help to modernise the postgraduate training of doctors. The NHS Medical Training Application Service ('MTAS', the system to apply for MMC posts) has recently come against severe national and international criticism. The perceived over-complexities, the rapidity of introduction, the lack of protection of personal data were some issues. The system was terminated, and the 'Tooke' enquiry (see later) was instituted in order to assess future planning. Contrary to some misconceptions, the latter enquiry has not recommended 'cancelling MMC' in order to revert to the training strategies of the past. The recommendations have broadly re-emphasised the role of 'core training' and 'higher training'.

Advantages of MMC:

- It provides a more structured training program to junior doctors especially in the earlier years of their post medical school training.
- There is now greater emphasis on training in the workplace, rather than purely theory.
- The training programmes will follow a set curriculum to ensure junior doctors receive a more predictable postgraduate education.
- Will produce Consultants on average about two years quicker than the old system.

Disadvantages of MMC:

- Junior doctors will need to make the decision regarding their chosen specialty after only two postgraduate years.
- Therefore it is of concern that if doctors are unable to gain adequate experience in some specialties, they will be less inclined to embark on these careers, and these particular specialties will have a shortage of trainees.
- Foreign doctors may have more difficulty in demonstrating competency in the new framework.
- Some are of the opinion that the rapid escalation to Consultant level coupled with the restrictions in working hours posed by the EWTD will result in less experienced newly qualified Consultants.

Questions one may be asked:

• What is your understanding of MMC?

• Do you think MMC is a good thing?

• What are the advantages/disadvantages of MMC?

• How will MMC affect your specialty?

• How would you ensure satisfactory training in your specialty?

• Will future Consultants in your specialty be as equipped to cope as they are at present?

• Has the 'Tooke' enquiry changed the plans for MMC?

Hospital at Night (HAN)

This was first proposed as a way of helping to comply with EWDT, and also maintain effective clinical care within the NHS. The project was first based around the concerns regarding the effects long working hours were having on junior doctors within the Deanery.

The aim of HAN is to have a multi-disciplinary team which has the full range of skills to provide immediate care to patients at night and the idea is that the MDT can handle emergencies for a variety of specialties. The team may be co-ordinated by a senior nurse, such as a clinical site manager. This structure allows the reduction in numbers of junior doctors at night, without compromising the quality of care provided.

The HAN scheme was initially piloted in 11 hospital trusts in 2004.

The principles of HAN are:

- To give more responsibilities normally conducted by doctors to non-medical staff, especially nurses.
- To reduce the amount of administration and duplication of tasks.
- To increase the effectiveness of multi disciplinary teams which are assembled based on competency rather than grades.

Examples of advantages of HAN to patients:

- Effective prioritisation of patients' needs through risk assessment.
- Increased co-ordination of care between medical, nursing and other staff.
- Allows the appropriate clinician to treat the patient in a timely way, without going through the irrelevant procedure of calling the 'patient's doctor first'.

Examples advantages of HAN to doctors:

- Improved teamworking during out-of-hours periods.
- Reduced isolation of healthcare professionals and improved morale at night.
- Reduced impact of long shifts on junior doctors.

Examples of disadvantages of HAN:

- Increased assessment of competencies are required.
- The relevance of recent specialty interventions are at times not appreciated by non-specialists (for example in a patient post-colo-rectal surgery, with an anastomotic leak leading to

pneumonia, the pneumonia may be treated without regard to the surgical aetiology). This may be overcome with satisfactory communication with the specialist teams out of hours and the following morning.

Questions you may be asked relating to HAN are:
- We have an active HAN service in our Trust – do you know much about HAN? What are the advantages/disadvantages of HAN?
- Do you think HAN has achieved the goals it originally intended to?
- Is your experience of HAN positive or negative? Why?
- Has HAN improved the lot of patients in your specialty?

European Working Time Directive (EWTD)
This is a directive from the Council of the European Union to protect the health and safety of workers within the European Union. It lays down minimum requirements for working hours, rest periods, annual leave and working arrangements for night workers. The Directive was enacted in UK law as 'Working Time Regulations', which took effect in 1 October 1998.

The regulations place a legal requirement on employers and build on the progress already made through the New Deal. The regulations are also part of wider aims to improve the work/life balance for NHS employees.

The main features of the EWTD are:

- Doctors can work no more than 48 hours work per week (averaged over a reference period).
- Doctors must have 11 hours continuous rest in a given 24 hour period.

- Doctors must have 24 hours continuous rest in seven days (or 48 hours in 14 days).
- Doctors must have a 20 minute break in work periods of over six hours.
- Doctors must have four weeks annual leave.
- Doctors working nights must not average more than eight hours work within 24 hours over the reference period.

The EWTD initially applied to all workers with a few exceptions, including doctors in training. From August 2004 it was extended to apply to these exceptions. This will be phased in with a maximum hours requirement reducing from 58 hours (which was implemented in 2004) to 48 hours in 2009.

SiMAP Judgement
The SiMAP judgement refers to a case brought before the European Court of Justice on behalf of a group of Spanish doctors. The ruling declared that all time spent by residents on-call would count as working time.

Jaeger Ruling
The European Court of Justice Judgement on Jaeger followed the SiMAP line. The implications of the Jaeger judgement are that staff who are required as part of their duties to be resident in hospital or other place of work out of hours and who are provided with on-call facilities are considered to be 'working' during their period of duty. The whole of the resident on-call period counts as working time whether or not the member of staff is working.

Staff who are off-site, non-resident on-call or who are not required to be continuously present at the hospital or other place of work are not considered to be working unless called to do so.

Questions one may be asked regarding EWTD:

- How has the EWTD affected the way in which junior doctors practice in your specialty?

- How has the EWTD affected the way in which Consultants practice in your specialty?

- What is your opinion on EWTD?

- Can you think of any innovations in your speciality which would allow us to implement EWTD better?

Chapter 17 Key points:

- BMA

- Royal Colleges

- MMC

- HAN

- EWTD

- Intricate facts are not important, though facts relevant to your specialty are!

Leadership and Management

Chapter 18 Principles of Leadership and Management for Doctors

For doctors in the past, the possession of leadership skills were taken for granted. Authority was implicit in the job, and there were very few issues which the Consultant had to justify or fight for. Often, major decisions affecting patient care and finances would be dealt with whimsically, without recourse. Leadership courses were not perceived to be needed; to the contrary, arrogance was the main characteristic levied at Consultants.

These days, we live in times of numerous targets and standards which have been set by Government. These are designed to have the best interest of the patient and NHS at heart, and are clearly not negotiable at a local level. Here, a significant impact can only be made at a regional or national forum. A key skill, therefore, is for the Consultant to identify issues which may be influenced at a Trust level, and to be able to use high quality leadership and management skills in order to achieve the best result for the patient and institution.

Although the distinction between 'leadership' and 'management' is often arbitrary, one should note the flavour of 'innovation', 'influence', 'inspiration' and 'vision' associated with the former, while 'facilitation' is strongly related to the latter. Clearly, many leaders are also managers and vice versa.

Most would agree that the non-clinical skills that incumbent Consultants and senior managers look for in a new colleague (and in an interviewee) involve management and leadership awareness. This is reflected in the nature of the questions. Topics already covered, and others yet to be discussed, include national politics, national bodies, financial structure, local Trust board structure, measures for standards, national and local finance, risk, complaints, ethics and legal issues. These are all 'management' topics.

Management

Doctors of all levels of seniority, from Foundation Year to senior Consultant, have responsibility for running teams, departments, directorates or Trusts. They should all aspire to drawing upon available resources in order to play some role in setting and developing priorities, and to make other decisions to improve the provision of healthcare in a given situation. Therefore all doctors have an obligation to be aware of the principles of effective management and to work effectively in a multi-disciplinary setting. Doctors are perfectly placed to provide management skills; they have the clinical knowledge, around which most strategic decisions are made; often, one Consultant is able to formulate a management plan, whereas a handful of managers is required to achieve the same aim. Unfortunately, the converse may apply: doctors may make poor managers if they feel that 'they are too important to manage', 'they are too busy performing clinical duties to manage'; the risk here is that unhappy doctors who do not engage in management duties are often left in sub-optimal situations, without having the tools to make things improve.

The GMC and management: definition and principles

The GMC definition of management in healthcare is:

> *'Getting things done well through and with people, creating an environment in which people can perform as individuals and yet co-operate towards achieving group goals, and removing obstacles to such performance.'*

The GMC also quotes seven principles of management for doctors:

- Selflessness
- Integrity
- Objectivity
- Accountability
- Openness
- Honesty
- Leadership.

Leadership

Leadership forms an integral part of effective management. Leadership may be defined in a number of ways:

- To guide and inspire others by persuasion or argument.
- To show the way by going first.
- To lead by setting an example to move forward.
- To change, and to test changes.

Humility, courage, realism and passion are characteristics often possessed by respected leaders. On the contrary, leadership should never embrace victimisation.

Questions one may be asked regarding leadership and management:

- Are you a leader?
- What makes a good leader?
- What leadership skills have you developed during your career?
- What do you understand by the term 'Leading by example'?
- What is management?
- Do you think doctors make good managers? Why?
- Can you recall a time when you had to demonstrate accomplished leadership qualities?
- How would you approach an under performing colleague?
- What leadership skills would you use to improve standards in your specialty?

Effective Team-working

Working as part of a team is vital for delivering effective treatment to patients. All doctors must demonstrate an appreciation of the characteristics of a good team and seek themselves to be good team players. The key points to working effectively within a medical team are:

- Clear understanding of the overall goals of the team.
- Clear understanding of your own individual responsibilities within the team.
- Ability to clearly communicate with your team members.
- Ability to listen to the views of the other team members.

Many aspects of healthcare require doctors and other healthcare professionals to work together. Effective teams are the means by which good, sustainable results are obtained. The medical profession has been increasingly keen to involve people from all clinical backgrounds in order to work effectively together in meeting shared goals for patients. As Trusts seek to become more flexible in the face of rapid change and more responsive to the needs of patients, they are experimenting with new, team-based approaches (for example, Hospital at Night).

Many skills are needed for teamwork, including:

- Effective communication
- Listening
- Questioning
- Persuading
- Respecting
- Helping
- Sharing of effort and values.

Questions you might be asked regarding teamwork:

- Give an example of how a complex clinical or managerial problem was solved through teamwork/deteriorated through lack of teamwork?
- How many multidisciplinary teams have you worked within in the last few months?
- Can you recall a time when you achieved a clinical or managerial goal through effective communication?
- Tell us about a team you have helped to organise – what went well and what went badly?
- Would you describe yourself as a leader or a follower?
- What are the advantages and disadvantages of a doctor leading a multidisciplinary team?

- Should a medical team rely on one leader?
- What is your opinion of giving nurses more responsibility in their role, in your specialty?

Chapter 18 Key points:

- History of leadership and doctors.

- Leadership versus management.

- Vital skills for Consultants equate to main topics for interview questions.

- Some principles of management.

- Some principles of leadership.

- Team-working and effective communication.

Chapter 19 The Trust Board structure and Trust Finances

The Trust Board

The Trust Board is the ultimate source of authority in the Trust and gives the overall sense of direction and purpose to the Trust's activities. It is headed by a non-executive Chairman, who is often part-time. There are in addition non-executive directors drawn from the local community, and sometimes from the Trust itself. The Executive Directors are headed by the Chief Executive.

The Executive Directors usually consist of the following:

- Chief Executive
- Medical Director
- Deputy Medical Director
- Workforce and Communications
- Finance and Information
- Chief Nurse
- Chief Operating Officer
- Director of Strategy and Planning
- The Deputy Chief Executive will either be permanent or the role may be used on an 'as needs' basis.

Organisational structure of the Trust Board

The structure and accountability tree will vary to some degree from Trust to Trust.

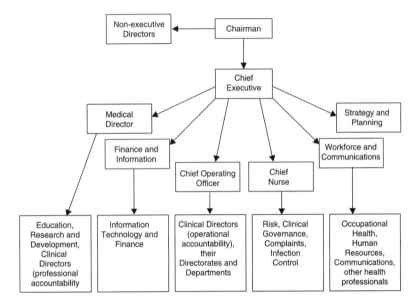

Core functions of the Trust Board

- Planning
- Standards and Performance
- Delegation: the right people in the right place to implement policies
- Finances
- Patient-centred.

The Board normally meets regularly (e.g. bi-monthly)

The Directorate structure

The Directorate structure continues to rapidly evolve. The original simple system consisted of an amalgamation of Departments or specialties with some relationship with each other; all doctors within the Directorate, including Consultants, would be accountable to the Clinical Director, while 'everyone else' within the Directorate would be accountable to the other figurehead, the General Manager (also known as an 'operational manager'). These old values have by and large been superseded.

In some Trusts, the label of 'Directorate' has been replaced by other terms, for instance 'Clinical Units' or 'Clinical Business Units', which is still nominally headed by the General/Operational Manager. This in turn would be sub-divided into 'groupings', which may be single specialty/departments, or slightly larger groups. These 'groupings' may rather strangely be called 'directorates' in some Trusts, and this nomenclature may cause some confusion for those still familiar with the pre-existing system. The 'groupings' or 'directorates' each have a clinical lead, who may be labelled as 'Clinical Directors'. The latter are *operationally* accountable to the General Manager. The Clinical Director is also *operationally* accountable to the Chief Operating Officer for higher-level issues, and *professionally* accountable to the Medical Director.

These changes have been implemented to give the 'groupings/directorates' and Clinical Directors more power (including budgetary power) in order to implement change, for clinical benefit. Somewhat paradoxically, this has also created a system where the Clinical Directors report to two non-medical individuals, where previously they often only reported to the Medical Director.

The old Directorate system:

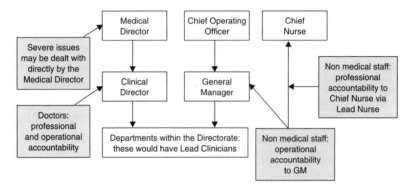

The new 'Clinical Unit' system:

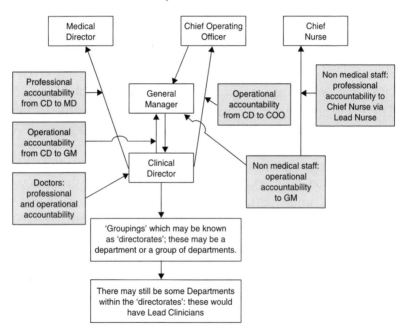

The day to day management of the Trust

This is often undertaken by Groups, such as:

- Strategic Investment Group.

- Financial and Performance Review Group.

- Operational Steering Group.

- It is perceived that the Clinical Directors play a greater role in managing the Trust than previously.

Questions you may be asked with regard to the Trust Board:

- Do you think that the 'Directorate' system works for your specialty?

- Do you think it is reasonable that senior doctors such as Clinical Directors should report to non-medical managers?

- If appointed, how could you improve the profile of your specialty within the Trust Board?

- Could you give us an example of issues that you would discuss with your Clinical Director/General Manager/Chief Operating Officer?

Many doctors have objections to the supposed indignity of reporting to non-medical managers. It should be clear, however, that this system works well when the doctor and the manager know which aspects are 'operational' issues, and which are 'professional'. The former are discussed with the Clinical Director and General Manager (and if sufficiently important, with the Chief Operating Officer), while the latter need to be discussed with the Clinical Director (and the Medical Director if sufficiently important). As many issues have both operational and professional components, the Clinical Director is well placed to handle these, and to liaise with the General Manager and appropriate Executive.

Departments with good operational strategies (for example with regard to outpatient non-attendees, complaints and risk) work well and develop a high profile within the Trust. On occasions these strategies may need to be recognised by the Clinical Director, General Manager and Chief Operating Officer, and applied to other areas in the Trust, via the Trust Board.

The following are a few high profile examples of 'operational' issues:

- Risk
- Complaints
- Finances and impact on Department, Directorate, Clinical Unit, Trust
- Professional conduct
- Education and training
- Clinical audit.

Contracts for the Trust and understanding with the Primary Care Trust

Long Term Service Agreements (LTSA), including a five year plan is devised. This involves detailed discussions between the Chief Executive of the Trust, additional Trust delegates and PCT commissioners. Topics for discussions include:

- Standards
- Cost and volume of Trust activity (based on Healthcare Resource Group analyses/'Payment by Results' and block tariffs)
- The development of existing partnerships and integrated care pathways.

There should be transparent dialogue between the Trust Board, clinicians and users. Regular reports pertaining to the LTSA should be available from the Chief Executive. The latter should incorporate:

- Strategy and annual plan
- Prioritisation.

Payments by Results and Healthcare Resource Groups have been dealt with in a previous chapter.

Chapter 19 Key points:

- Trust Board

- Organisational structure

- Core functions

- Day to day management

- Know the reporting structure and the difference between operational and professional issues

- Well-managed Departments have a high profile within the Trust Board

- Long Term Service Agreement.

Chapter 20 Some additional qualities required of a Consultant

The vital qualities of leadership and management have been discussed in a previous chapter.

Providing appraiser services (the principles of appraisal have been discussed in a previous chapter)

It is essential that the appraiser has a good working knowledge of what constitutes practice development of the doctor being appraised. An important question to ask is 'what can this trust do to improve your practice development?' It is not essential that the appraiser is a Clinical Director or a Lead Clinician. In fact it is perhaps an advantage that this is not the case, so that the issues of service provision and appraisal are not confused. However when appraising, it is important to recognise when an issue had an impact not only on appraisal, but also on validation and service provision. One example of such an issue is rudeness to patients. In these cases the appraiser should simply deal with the appraising issue, and organise further meetings to deal with validation and Trust management. It would be prudent for potential appraisers to attend appraiser courses.

It is not vital that job planning (see below) runs concurrently with appraisal, however it should be clearly understood that any changes in the structure of a job for the benefit of practice development may lead to changes in planned activities.

Questions which may be asked (taken from previous chapter):

• What is the difference between appraisal and validation?

• If we were to appoint you, who would you expect to appraise you, and how often? What particular topics do you think you ought to be appraised on?

• Do you think that the current Consultant appraisal process is satisfactory? Is it just a 'tick box' interview? How do you think we can improve the quality of appraisals for Consultants?

Issues relating to discipline and validation of a doctor and colleague

It is important to differentiate between issues of simple feedback (for example for minor substandard behaviour) and those for formal discipline. One-to-one feedback sessions should be seen by all concerned as productive. It is important not to label or imply that any informal feedback sessions dealing with difficulties are 'disciplinary', as the latter carries significant implications. It may even be appropriate to minute an informal chat and provide the individual with a written summary of this. In situations of a doctor's substandard practice, informal meetings and correspondence may become more common as all individuals and institutions have some responsibility to contribute to the practice development of the doctor and future protection of patients and other institutions when the doctor moves on.

When it is clear that the behaviour of a doctor will lead to a Trust disciplinary hearing, plans should be made. The meeting should be announced to the individual doctor, who then has a chance to be accompanied by legal and union representatives. The Trust should make a decision as to who should attend this meeting; it may seem sensible to include relevant healthcare professionals, operational managers, medical personnel and executive representation. It may also be prudent to include the doctor's college tutor.

When there are repercussions with regard to a threat to validation, this fitness to practice issue should be dealt with by formal correspondence to the GMC. A copy of this correspondence needs to be sent to all individuals responsible for appraising the doctor. When a case is being assessed by the GMC, this needs to be declared at appraisals and interviews.

Questions which may be asked:
- A scenario relating to substandard practice in a colleague.
- What features in a colleague's behaviour would make you consider organising a disciplinary hearing, as opposed to an informal discussion?
- What features in a colleague's behaviour would impact on fitness to practise?

The 'new' Consultant Contract and Job Planning
Clearly, the practice development needs highlighted in appraisal meetings need to be reflected in the job plan; for this reason, appraisal and job planning often go hand in hand. Both of these procedures need to occur at least annually.

From 31 October 2003, incumbent Consultants had the option of taking up the new contract or remaining on their current terms and conditions. All appointments to consultant posts first advertised after 31 October were offered only on the terms of the new contract. The aim of the change was to satisfactorily remunerate Consultants for the work they did in the NHS, while ensuring that the working time was carefully accounted for.

The new contract converted periods of duty (fours hours during the working week, and three during the weekend) into 'programmed activities' (PAs). An average of 40 hours per week, therefore, would equate to ten PAs.

The PA's would be divided into:

- Direct clinical care (DCC): this would include 'hands on' clinical care, including inpatient work, outpatient work and ward rounds. Many institutions allow DCCs for dictation of clinic letters.
- Supported programmed activities (SPA): this would include general administration, clinical audit, education for trainees, self-education (translating into 'Continuing Professional Development' (CPD) points) and research.

For 'on call' work out of hours, the 'predictable' duties, such as weekend ward rounds and residential on-call, are remunerated as PAs. 'Unpredictable' duties, such as being available for discussion and occasionally being physically present during on-call, are remunerated as a (small) flat fee annexed to the salary.

Most new posts are advertised as 'ten PA' posts. For purposes of cost and equity, there is a lot of pressure on Trusts to regulate the number of PAs paid to Consultants, and to confirm that the numbers are genuine. The usual recommendation is that 75 per cent of PAs are DCCs, while 25 per cent are SPAs. It should be emphasised that this breakdown is only an understanding, and often is not adhered to.

Questions which may be asked:

- Do you know much about the Consultant contract (previously known as the 'new' Consultant contract)?

- How often would you expect to partake in Job Planning sessions, and with whom?

- What would we expect of you for your SPAs/how can we guarantee value for money for your SPAs?

- Do you think it is acceptable that Consultants may engage in SPA's from home?

The point of these questions is the perception that many Consultants are paid significant sums of money for 'management', 'teaching' and 'reading journals', without there being any objective way of measuring output. This in turn may lead to resentment among managerial and other non-medical staff. The answer lies in creating a professional and accurate log of activities, such as timetabled teaching, meetings with managers and internal/external CPDs. Clinical audit projects (title, your role, status of project) should be formally logged. These details may then be discussed at the Job Planning session with your Clincal Director. It may be reasonable in the future that SPA's would be allocated purely on the productivity of these items, rather than there being an 'automatic' allocation which is perceived to belong to the Consultant 'by right'. Some Trusts are quite relaxed about the engagement of SPAs from home, on the understanding that productivity is guaranteed.

Standards of business conduct

All doctors should act in their patients' interests, and this should supersede all other interests. They should be impartial, and there should never be an abuse of position.

Gifts should never be acceptable in order to induce action. When gifts are accepted, these should be logged with the General Manager. Money is never acceptable. Hospitality (for instance from the pharmaceutical industry) should be broadly similar to Trust quality. If this is not, the offer should be logged or declined. Where there is Commercial sponsorship for meetings or posts, there should be no inducement for the purchase of relevant products.

All doctors should declare any involvement with services which compete with the Trust, and also any outside employment/interest which conflicts with Trust duties.

In the event that a doctor devises or invents a clinical product while in Trust employment, the intellectual property rights for the article(s) are transferred to the Trust. The inventor status remains with the doctor, and royalties for the article(s) may be negotiated by the Trust and the doctor.

The attire of doctors is attracting a lot of debate. The public have, over the decades, become used to the pin-striped suit and the white coat. These days, however, where cleanliness and drug-resistant organisms are high on the agenda for the public and the Department of health, it is not surprising that there are pressures exerted on the Trust by the Department of Health to review the clothing of doctors and Consultants. The initiative of 'bare below the elbows' is understood by many to be a sensible approach to clinical work, to aid hand washing; cynics point to the lack of evidence for patient benefit. This issue may become a very good example of a dictat which may only be negotiable at the level of Department of Health (that is, at Trust level it is not negotiable).

Questions which may be asked:

- Scenario question, pertaining to a gift/money from a relative.
- Do you agree with the 'bare below the elbows' strategy?
- How could you convince your colleagues to comply with the 'bare below the elbows' directive?

How to Develop a Service or submit a 'Business Case'

It may be that an extension to a Departmental service is planned in your specialty. Indeed you may have been short listed as a result of possessing specific clinical attributes pertaining to the development. The Panel will want to see that you are able to be a key player in these developments.

Even if there are no developments afoot, the Panel will want to see that you will be able to submit a high quality bid for new facilities, taking into account the Trust's finances and predicament with regard to the PCT and other external pressures such as the Healthcare Commission.

The basic principles with regard to making a business case/ 'bid' are:

- Establish a case of need.
- Devise a business plan.
- Secure funding.
- Implement the plan effectively, with named individuals and roles.
- Review implementation for desired goals at agreed intervals.

Establishing a case of need can be identified by:

- Speaking to colleagues and gaining their opinion.

- Gaining feedback from patient focus groups.

- Analysing any recommendations drawn from previously conducted audits or authoritative external assessments.

- Comparing your new department's practice against others.

- Correlate with the Trust's pressures and anxieties e.g. patient satisfaction, inpatient/outpatient/surgical targets.

Once you have identified a case of need, a business plan for service delivery is then needed. A clearly presented business plan will be used by the decision makers in their considerations as to whether the proposal is credible, achievable and cost effective.

The business plan will:

- Explain why a service of this type is required.

- Justify why the service should be implemented.

- Clearly illustrate the cost versus benefits – e.g. reduce waiting times, save money, improve healthcare provision.

- If possible, factor in a risk assessment of implementing the service and not implementing the service.

- Provide a detailed step by step plan as to how the proposal will be implemented.

- Make recommendations as to who could fund the proposal.

It is important that the plan is not seen as over-optimistic.

Funding options – there are three main options:

- Additional support funding provided by the local NHS commissioners (the local NHS Primary Care Trust).

- Monies from identified charities or donations.

- Monies released by closing or reducing a current service.

Questions which may be asked:

- How would you contribute to the planned expansion of your specialty?

- What non-clinical skills do you have which would facilitate the development of your specialty?

- What qualities does a successful business case have?

- How would you contribute to establishing a new service, or an extension to an existing service, within the department you are hoping to join?

Data handling

It is the duty of every doctor to use and handle patient data (electronic or otherwise) in a professional way. The Data Protection Act in 1984 suggested that all data should be:

- Relevant

- Accurate

- Updated

- Processed formally

- Not for disclosure

- Kept only as long as necessary

- Accessible to the patient who has eventual rights to access and amendment

- Secure.

In 2002 NPfIT suggested that each Trust should have named custodian(s) to ensure confidentiality. There should be strict terms of internet usage with relevance to context, browsing and software. On applying security, there should be appropriate facilities for data storage and passwords. Patient access should be facilitated by an application in writing to the Data

Protection Coordinator of the Trust. It should be remembered that it also applies to information about health care professionals, research projects and corporate issues.

Joint Guidance on Protecting Electronic Patient Information from the BMA and NHS Connecting for Health (CFH)

- Everyone in the NHS has a responsibility to understand the implications of dealing with electronic patient data.
- Signpost key guidance so that each individual and organisation is aware of their responsibilities in protecting patient information.

1. The NHS Code of Confidentiality

- Always log-out of any computer system or application when work on it is finished and do not leave a terminal unattended and logged-in.
- Do not share logins with other people and do not reveal passwords to others.
- Change passwords at regular intervals and avoid using obvious passwords.
- Always clear the screen of a previous patient's information before seeing another.
- Use a password-protected screen-saver to prevent casual viewing of patient information by others.

2. Organisational responsibilities

- Each organisation should have security, information governance and records management policies in place, which should be endorsed by the Board or senior partners and updated at regular intervals.

- Organisations must complete the Information Governance Toolkit which measures progress against a series of standards.

- Each organisation is also required to complete an information governance statement of compliance, which ensures that organisations that use NHS CFH services meet certain standards.

- Organisations must ensure that staff are aware of good practice with regard to security.

- Staff members should receive regular training including:

  ○ What information they are using, how it should be used and how it should be protectively handled, stored and transferred, including outputs from computer systems.

  ○ What procedures, standards and protocols exist for the sharing of information with relevant others and on a 'need to know' basis.

  ○ How to report a suspected or actual breach of information security within the organisation, or to an affected external information service provider or to a partner organisation.

3. NHS Connecting for Health's Responsibilities

- Smartcards – Access to the NHS Care Records Service will eventually only be possible using a Smartcard and an alpha numeric pass code.

- Legitimate Relationships – Patient records should only be accessed by those with a legitimate relationship.

- Role-Based Access – The elements of a record, which can be accessed, will be dependent on the role of the staff member and this is set up on registration.

• Audit trails and alerts – Access to the NHS Care Records Service will be audited and alerts will be triggered to highlight possible inappropriate access.

4. NHS responsibilities

• The NHS Care Record Guarantee provides a commitment that the patient's records will be used in ways that respect their rights to secure, confidential and accurate records.

 There are 12 commitments, which include:

• Records will be shared with healthcare teams on a 'need to know' basis.

• Identifiable healthcare information will not be shared with other government agencies unless permission has been granted, it is required by law, or approval has been granted for health or research purposes under section 251 of the NHS Act 2006.

• Agreement will be obtained before sharing information with other external organisations such as social services or education.

• Patients can limit how their information is shared.

The Freedom of Information Act 2000

This received Royal Assent on 30 November 2000. It gave a right of access to all types of recorded information held by public authorities and placed obligations on public authorities to disclose information, subject to a range of exemptions. In common with other public bodies, NHS Professionals were required to implement the Act fully from January 2005, when access rights came into force. This enabled anyone to make a request for information, although the request had to be in writing (letter, fax or e-mail). The Act gave applicants two related rights: the right to be told whether the information exists; the right to receive the information within 20 working days, where possible in the manner requested.

Questions you may be asked:
- How would you ensure that patient data was adequately protected?
- Can you identify any problems with data handling in your specialty?
- How could you improve your service using electronic patient data?
- There may be a scenario concerning transferring patient data using non-institution e-mail services.
- Do you think that the Freedom of Information Act has benefited patients and healthcare professionals in your specialty?

Dealing with the media

All issues relating to the involvement and presence of media within the Trust must be discussed with the Press and Communication Department in the Trust. This applies not only to VIP visits but also to the involvement of professional groups such as Royal colleges. The trust must ensure that patient consent is achieved when appropriate. High profile patients must be afforded the same dignity and confidentiality given to all other patients.

Chapter 20 Key points:

- Principles of appraising.

- Issues relating to discipline and validation of a doctor and colleague.

- Awareness of the Consultant Contract and the principles of job planning.

- Standards of business: behaviour, gifts, attire.

- Developing a service and submitting a business case.

- Patient data awareness and handling.

- Dealing with the media.

Chapter 21 Clinical Governance

Although clinical governance in the NHS has probably existed in some form or another for decades, its history probably formally began in 1998 when the Department of Health published 'A first class service: quality in the NHS'. This set out for the first time the Government's policy for raising quality for NHS patients and services. The policy involved setting standards through the National Institute for Clinical Excellence and the national service frameworks, and monitoring standards through the Commission for Health Improvement, patient forums and national patient satisfaction surveys. Central to this process would be delivering higher quality services through better self-regulation and through clinical governance. 'A first class service' gave a complex definition of clinical governance: 'A framework through which NHS organisations are accountable for continuously improving the quality of their services and safeguarding high standards of care, by creating an environment in which excellence in clinical care will flourish'.

More recently the focus of clinical governance has expanded significantly in the light of reports such as 'Organisation with a memory' (1999), the Kennedy report on Bristol children's hospital (2001), the Toft report on intrathecal chemotherapy (2001) and 'Building a safer NHS for patients' (2001). These, and the launch of the National Patient Safety Agency in September, have mapped out the quality agenda in terms of the

NHS plan's objective of a patient-centred NHS. In addition,
the National Health Service Reform and Health Care Professionals Bill spells out even more clearly that in future
professional bodies will have to focus on improving their
systems to involve more lay people and re-emphasise their role
in protecting patients and the public.

Key principles include:

- Framework for quality and standards in the right
  environment.
- Accountable, safe, open, questioning.
- Relevant to everyone.
- Important components:
  ○ Quality assurance, clinical effectiveness and openness
  ○ Risk management
  ○ Complaints
  ○ Clinical audit
  ○ Research and development
  ○ Education and training and continuing professional
    development.

Although these components used to be thought of as 'pillars'
of clinical governance, it should now be understood that every
aspect of clinical work has an impact on, and is associated
with, the concept of clinical governance. The risk associated
with the identification and listing of specific components is
that of misunderstanding the philosophy of clinical governance, and missing vital components which may not be on a
'list'.

Clinical governance is becoming such a popular topic that
there may be many candidates who are now in a position to
provide satisfactory stock answers in an interview. It is

important to recognise, therefore, that interviewers are keen to identify candidates who are able to identify specific examples of ways in which any or all of the components in Clinical Governance may be used to improve standards for patients, the Trust and providers of health care.

In addition it should be noted that there are several meetings which encompass clinical governance; for instance forums dealing with complaints, risk, clinical audit and research are all technically 'clinical governance' meetings. This is often forgotten when asked 'how many clinical governance meetings have you attended recently?'

Questions you may be asked relating to clinical governance include:

- What do you know about Clinical Governance?
- How does Clinical Governance deal with patient safety?
- How does Clinical Governance impact on your daily work?
- Do you think Clinical Governance is useful or is it just another layer of bureaucracy?
- Are there any problems with the way Clinical Governance is implemented?
- Who, in your hospital, is responsible for Clinical Governance?
- What is Clinical Risk Management?
- What is a Near-Miss situation?
- What happens to Critical Incident Forms once they have been submitted?
- How many clinical governance meetings have you attended recently?
- How many risk meetings have you attended recently?

- If we appointed you how would you run clinical governance in your specialty?

Clinical governance consistently and perpetually influences every aspect of day-to-day care in the NHS. Dealing with clinical risk impacts greatly on patient safety, and this is a vital ingredient for the provision of a good quality clinical service. It is vital that everyone within the Trust is aware of the relevant individuals leading teams in risk, complaints, clinical audit, research and training/education. Knowledge of what happens to an adverse incident form is vital, as is knowledge of the risk/adverse event-feedback process. It is highly recommended that all departments and specialties run regular meetings where all the topics of clinical governance may be openly discussed.

Chapter 21 Key points:

- Be aware of the history of clinical governance, and know the important components.

- Do not see clinical governance as a specific 'list' or 'pillars'; appreciate the heterogeneous ways that standards may be improved.

- If asked about clinical governance in an interview, try to think of specific examples where interventions may improve standards.

- There are many meetings which may come under the remit of 'clinical governance' e.g. clinical audit, research.

- Be aware of the key individuals that help run departments important to clinical governance (e.g. risk, complaints, clinical audit, research, training/education).

- Be prepared to volunteer to run regular clinical governance meetings in your department/specialty.

Chapter 22 Quality assurance, clinical effectiveness and openness

Quality assurance

This term may be applied to any intervention, measurement, target or mechanism which may contribute to the improvement in the quality of health care services. Examples include:

- Service benefits and targets: reducing the length of hospital stays, estimated caseloads, complaints procedures.
- Audit arrangements: frequency of reporting, reporting route and format, dissemination mechanisms.
- Clinical quality criteria: appropriateness of treatment, waiting times.
- Patient satisfaction: developing and improving support in the hospital and community.
- Patient outcomes: improving health related quality of life.
- Information requirements: including both patient-specific information (NHS number, referring GP) and service-specific information (workload trends, number of complaints).
- The process for reviewing the service with stakeholders, including decisions on changes necessary to improve or to decommission a service.

Questions which may be asked:
- If you were to develop a new service, how would you measure its impact?
- How would you measure quality in your specialty?

Clinical effectiveness

Clinical effectiveness is a measure of the extent to which a particular intervention works. This assessment should include whether the intervention is appropriate and whether it represents value for money. In the modern health service, clinical practice needs to be perpetually refined in the light of ever-emerging evidence of effectiveness but also has to consider aspects of efficiency and safety from the perspective of the individual patient and carers in the wider community. These issues are often discussed in clinical governance meetings, clinical audit meetings and research meetings.

Questions which may be asked:
- What is your understanding of the term 'clinical effectiveness'?
- How many meetings dealing with clinical effectiveness have you attended recently?

Openness

Poor performance and poor practice can too often thrive behind closed doors. Processes which are open to public scrutiny, while respecting individual patient and practitioner confidentiality, and which can be justified openly, are an essential part of quality assurance. Open proceedings and discussion about clinical governance issues should be a feature of any framework. Any organisation providing high quality care has to show that it is meeting the needs of the population it serves.

Openness in turn may lead to co-operation between Trust and NHS organisations.

Questions which may be asked:

• Have you attended any meetings recently which could be more open to external scrutiny?

• With regard to clinical governance issues, do you think openness is important? Why?

Chapter 22 Key points:

• Quality assurance: Any intervention, measurement, target or mechanism which may contribute to the improvement.

• Clinical effectiveness: A measure of the extent to which a particular intervention works. Consider appropriateness, value for money, evidence, efficiency and safety.

• Openness: Essential part of quality assurance. Exposes poor practice. Demonstrates quality of care, and whether the care meets the needs of the population it serves. This may improve co-operation between departments and organisations.

Chapter 23 Risk management and complaints

Adverse healthcare events and risk

As already discussed, an expert report on clinical risk was conducted by the Department of Health in 2000. This led to the white paper 'An organisation with a memory'. The main features of the report were:

- Uncommon

- Devastating consequences

- Costly consequences

- Familiar ring to most of the errors

- Often the picture was incomplete

- NHS was not good at learning lessons: when things went wrong an individual or individuals were identified to carry the blame. The focus of incident analysis had tended to be on the events immediately surrounding an adverse event, and in particular on the human acts or omissions immediately preceding the event itself.

- Common themes: medical devices, adverse reactions to drugs, mental health services committed suicide, hospital acquired infections.

The proposed way forward:

- The commitment of all NHS staff and the boards of all NHS organisations and Trusts; unified mechanisms were recommended for reporting, and analysis when things go wrong; the establishment of clear national and local mechanisms for reporting mistakes and near misses and analysing trends.
- A more open culture; the creation of a culture where staff feel that they can report errors, mistakes and adverse events without fear of retribution.
- Mechanisms for ensuring that the necessary changes were put into practice; the learning of lessons to reduce risk and prevent future harm to patient.
- A much wider appreciation of the value of the system approach in preventing, analysing and learning from errors.

Outcomes from the reports described above (see previous chapter):

- The National Patient Safety Agency (NPSA).
- Clinical Negligence Scheme for Trusts (CNST), administered by the NHS Litigation Authority (NHSLA).
- The National Reporting and Learning System (NRLS).
- An integrated approach to investigating errors across the NHS and different agencies.
- The following authorities developed relationships to the bodies above:
  - The National Clinical Assessment Authority – it is now part of the NPSA as National Clinical Assessment Service (NCAS).
  - The General Medical Council.
  - The Healthcare Commission.

Questions which may be asked:

- Have you had any dealings with your Trust's Risk Department? How does it work?

- How many types of meetings have you attended recently, which have dealt with clinical risk?

- Can you recall being involved in a clinical situation which involved clinical risk? How was it dealt with?

- How is risk dealt with in your present department or directorate?

- Have you ever filled in a 'Serious untoward incident' ('SUI') form? Whose hands did it go through? What actions did you take to follow up?

- Has your department any strong interfaces with the NPSA/ NRLS?

As mentioned in a previous chapter, the impact and interfaces of clinical risk is widespread. It is therefore ideal that most directorates and departments in the NHS aspire to holding regular multi-disciplinary meetings dedicated to clinical and non-clinical risk. Doctors should realise the importance of them, and attend. All Trusts and all directorates should have registers of clinical and non clinical risk. There should be evidence of consistent handling and cross-directorate learning.

It is vital that any 'adverse incident' forms are followed through. A thorough understanding is essential of: the type of personnel in the department responsible for risk; their responsibilities in dealing with adverse incidents; the process of actions; method of recommendations. It is good practice for the individuals responsible for submission of the adverse incident form to check the status of assessment. Conversely, the risk department should as a matter of course feed back to these individuals.

If the risk process is seen as a genuine tool for improving clinical effectiveness, and risk form submission leads to a note of thanks rather than blame from the Trust, the submission of forms to the risk department should rise in quality and number. The main philosophy of form submission should be that 'I can make things better by involving the risk team'. If the submission is thought to be inappropriate by the risk team, the response should be educational rather than dismissive.

It should be remembered that compliance with statutory regulations can help to minimise risks to patients. In addition, patient risks can be minimised by ensuring that systems are regularly reviewed and questioned – for example, by critical event audit and learning from complaints.

One should remember that risk also applies to health care practitioners and the Trust. A safe environment, availability of best evidence to practice and maintenance of quality assurance are paramount.

Complaints

The frequency of complaints in healthcare has been rising for a considerable number of years. Most would agree that whereas patients and relatives felt vulnerable, threatened and generally unable to complain in decades gone by, these days there are heterogeneous reasons to do so. Some merely use the process to seek an explanation. Others feel genuinely aggrieved, and wish to 'protect others'. On occasions the complaint is an expression of anger, grief or raised expectations. Rarely, it appears blatant that the complainant is simply seeking compensation. All these triggers are facilitated by a process which has been made easier for the complainant. Common reasons identified include staff attitude, lack of information, poor communication, appointments and generally poor care.

In the case of a verbal complaint, due attention and a quick resolution is in the interest of the complainant and all concerned. It should be recognised that the complaint may be verbally addressed to any individual, who indeed may not have any relationship to the complaint. However the latter has a duty to inform the complaint lead for the department; this may be the lead nurse or the matron. The group of relevant individuals need to be gathered, and a consensus needs to be formed as to the next strategy. Whether there is substance to the complaint or not, every effort needs to be made to provide an explanation to the complainant. This may be accompanied by an apology if it is understood that there has been a mistake. It is probable that a quick and empathetic response here will dramatically reduce the chances of a more formal complaint.

The above process may be repeated if any or all of the individuals are dissatisfied, and feel that some resolution may occur.

When a written (registered) complaint has been lodged, there is a set process which needs to be adhered to by the Trust. On receipt of the complaint, this is forwarded to the complaint lead. As in verbal complaints, the individual to whom the complaint is addressed may not be centrally or in any way involved with the case. The document is registered by the complaint lead, and the investigation begins with the organisation of statements from all relevant individuals. Once all the statements are completed, the outcome is concluded by way of an overall assessment by a delegated individual. This is often the Medical Director. A draft letter is created by the complaint lead, and this is signed and sent by the Chief Executive. The written responses by relevant individuals and that of the Chief Executive should be clear and in plain English. They should answer all the issues, and not be defensive. An apology should be made if there has been a clear error, and in these cases there should be action points to prevent reoccurrence. The whole process from receipt by the Trust of the complaint to the sending of the Chief Executive's response, should take no longer than 20 working days.

The written response from the Trust/Chief Executive may be rejected. It may be apparent at this stage whether further written correspondence and clarification from the Trust may be acceptable for the complainant.

If the latter is not acceptable, the next stage is the Independent Review. This is dealt with in the Trust by a panel of independent individuals external to the Trust, who have the expertise to make a decision. The panel is chaired by the Independent Lay Chair. In order for the review to occur, the reason for dissatisfaction needs to be clear, and the Independent Lay Chair needs to decide if the case is justified. If there does not seem to be justification, further local resolution may be advised. The Independent Review Panel (IRP) consists of the: convenor, Independent Lay Chair, independent lay panel member and two independent clinical advisors. These individuals are charged with reading the records, conducting the interview and providing a report. It is likely that the function of the IRP will cease to exist in the not too distant future, and that failed local written responses may then proceed directly to the Ombudsman.

If the findings of the IRP are considered not acceptable by the complainant, the next and final stage of the complaints process is the Ombudsman assessment. As in the IRP, this is independent of the Trust. The Ombudsman has affiliations with the Department of Health via the Healthcare Commission. The high profile of this organisation would suggest that this referral should be seen as a matter of last resort. A report and related recommendations and action points are created. The decision by the Ombudsman, whether the complaint is sustained or not, is final, and needs to be accepted by the complainant.

It should be remembered that the complaints procedures described above are quite separate from those of litigation, though clearly there are occasions when the two processes are closely linked. Therefore individuals who have either failed, or indeed have never entered into, the complaints process may embark upon legal avenues. The Clinical Negligence Scheme for Trusts (CNST) is a means by which Trusts may fund the costs of litigation, and provide effective management of claims. It is administered by the NHS Litigation Authority (NHSLA).

The Trust should see the complaints process as a vehicle that allows quality development, and the Complaints Department should have close ties to the risk management team.

Needless to say, all complainants have a requirement to behave appropriately. Abusive and violent behaviour from patients or relatives should not be tolerated, and all health care professionals have a right to work in a safe environment.

Questions you may be asked:

- Why do you think that the incidence of complaints is rising? Are you in a position to do anything about this within your specialty?

- Have you ever been involved (or know a colleague who has been involved) in a complaints process? Can you describe the sequence of events? Could anything have been done better?

- You may be given a scenario where a patient verbally informs you of a grievance, or a complainant hands you a written complaint.

Chapter 23 Key points:

- History of risk.

- The subsequent development of Trust strategies and national bodies associated with risk.

- Risk is a good tool to improve clinical and corporate effectiveness.

- Reasons for the rise in frequency of complaints.

- Processes for verbal and written complaints.

- Complaints should be used as a vehicle for quality development.

Chapter 24 Clinical audit and research

Clinical Audit

Definition and brief summary of Clinical Audit

Most would agree that the term 'Audit' is applied (wrongly) to a large range of activities. The Concise Oxford Dictionary suggests the 'Official examination of accounts or Account Book'. Many universities would, at the end of Deanery Accounting, have an Audit Feast, at which Audit Ale would be drunk. This would be chaired by the Chancellor or Rector. In 1956, *medical* audit became apparent and one early definition was the 'Evaluation of medical care in retrospect through analysis of clinical records ... to make certain that the full benefits of medical knowledge are being applied effectively to the needs of the patients' (Lembcke). In 1989 the Secretaries of State (chaired by Ken Clarke) suggested the 'Systematic, critical analysis of the quality of medical care, including the procedures used for diagnosis and treatment, the use of resources and the resulting outcome and quality of life for the patients'. In any case, a reasonable summary would be 'Quality assurance, with two caveats: a) led by health professionals and b) confidential to them'. Luckily, by being inclusive, we (clinical and non-clinical staff) all qualify for this. Furthermore, clinical audit is the process whereby clinical teams examine their practice by comparing the approaches they make with standards or guidelines. In short, a clinical audit is a study which sets out to answer the question – 'are we doing things right'?

Is Clinical Audit a cycle or a spiral? One could argue that topic selection, specification of desired performance, data collection, implementation of changes, further data collection, review of standards, and so on should lead to an ever upward and spiralling phenomenon.

Pressures and advantages for performing Clinical Audit

Audit is itemised in the Appraisal of Consultants. Junior doctors will often either have a requirement (from the Deanery) or a desire to partake in an audit project. By and large, non-medical staff find the experience of performing clinical audit enjoyable and career-enhancing. It should not be a requirement for any one individual to commence or finish an audit project in order to fulfil their appraisal/validation requirement. Evidence of involvement in a project should suffice. Each project therefore should have multiple auditors (kept to a sensible number) with a Lead Auditor. This should enhance teamwork, and obviate the perennial problem of exiting junior doctors and upcoming appraisals.

Participating Groups

Audit should be inclusive. The nature of the Groups should be listed, though the list should not be seen as comprehensive. Other than Directorates and Departments, Cross-Departmental examples include Nursing, Management, Therapeutics, Portering Services, Kitchen Services, Domestic Services and Security.

New guideline from an external credible source

When a new guideline becomes apparent (for example from NICE or NPSA) often through the Trust's risk department, the Clinical Audit/Clinical Effectiveness lead should cascade this to the relevant clinicians. In turn the clinicians should let the Clinical Audit/Clinical Effectiveness team know whether the new guideline should be incorporated by the Trust, or of any reasons for rejection of the guideline.

Types of triggers for Clinical Audit

I would propose a formal grading, to aid topic selection and the auditing of audits.

Type 1: Personal experience or impression that things could be done better (there should be an attempt to describe the deficiency).
Type 2: Adverse event.
Type 3: Awareness of a new guideline which should be followed; this may be from an external credible source or from within the Trust.

Implementation of findings (education)

Tried and variably trusted techniques include:

a) Feedback
b) Educational strategies
   - Materials
   - Conferences/seminars/workshops
   - Outreach visits by opinion leaders to Trusts, Departments and Directorates
   - Patient mediated. The strength and potential of this has not been widely implemented

- Self-efficacy: involvement of those who have a perception of 'lack of knowledge', together with practical support
- Inverse social facilitation: for those individuals thought not to care ('social loafers, free-riders'), make them accountable

c) Reminders
d) Organisational change
e) Combination of any or all of the above.

The stages involved in carrying out an audit are:

- Registration: Confirmation of the trigger; desired performance should be identified using a credible (named) source; estimation of the size of the impact (estimate of the size of the audited population and relevance of the standard); presentation date and venue decided; registration number issued.

- Data made available. The lead auditor should describe the methodology of inclusion/exclusion criteria and lost data. This should generally mirror the rigor of data handling in research projects.

- Commencement of data interpretation.

- Data analysis. Statistical methodology should be made clear.

- Data interpretation. Discrepancies and philosophies should be made clear e.g. Bp 'tick' (does this mean Bp normal or Bp performed?).

- Presentation with recommendations for implementation.

- Consider incorporating the standard into the Trust's 'Good Clinical Practice' or 'Protocol' register.

- Review post-implementation data.

- Re-audit.

If asked to illustrate a recent clinical audit project, one should describe the role (e.g. lead auditor), trigger, standard, impact, methodology (data collection, analysis and interpretation), presentation, recommendations and plans for education. It is often the description of the education strategies that is found wanting.

Questions you may be asked:
- What do you think the main benefit of clinical audit is?
- What methods would you use to implement the findings of your recent clinical audit project? What if there were perpetual problems in compliance?

Medical research

Medical research aims to improve the health of people by identifying new treatments and health care approaches, or by re-testing recent developments towards confirming or rejecting their value. Research performed by doctors may include clinical trials, laboratory based research or hypothesis-driven research through reviews of current literature. Most would agree that it is not essential for all doctors to participate in research. However, it is vital to recognise that the understanding of results from research projects are key to the implementation of good clinical practice, and the adoption of the principles of evidence based medicine (EBM).

Research governance

Any clinically-based research involving patients and volunteers must adhere to the following principles:

- The foreseeable risks must not outweigh the potential benefits.
- Ethical approval must be obtained prior to commencement.

- All volunteers involved in the research must be made fully aware of any potential risks.
- Consent must be obtained from all participants.
- The participants' confidentiality must be respected.
- Clinicians involved in the provision of healthcare to the participants, such as GPs, must be kept fully aware of the progress.
- The research project must be completed fully except where direct risk to the participants become apparent.
- All results arising from the research project must be recorded accurately.
- All actions and decisions must be able to be explained, justified and defended.

The implementation of research

Good professional practice has always sought to evolve in the light of evidence from research. The time lag for introducing such change can at times be long, and reducing this time lag requires emphasis on the implementation of research. The following techniques are vital for implementation:

- Critical appraisal of the literature in the presence of a group of relevant experts.
- Upon agreement by this group, commencement of 'project management' and the development of guidelines and protocols.
- Submission of the guideline or protocol to the Trust Board for approval. This is vital, as there may be cost or administrative implications. For example, a new drug may need to go through the Trust Drugs and Therapeutics Committee.

Evidence Based Medicine (EBM)

Evidence-Based Medicine differs from the conventional approach of relying on clinical reasoning from basic scientific fact, by using actual clinical evidence. For example if a clinical trial shows the effective prescribing of a particular class of drug with regard to a new condition, this philosophy takes preference over basic scientific principles.

The Centre for Evidence-Based Medicine defines EBM as 'the conscientious, explicit and judicious use of current best evidence in making decisions about the care of individual patients. The practice of evidence-based medicine means integrating individual clinical expertise with the best available external clinical evidence from systematic research.'

The key points when understanding, defining and implementing the principles of EBM are:

- Using the best available research evidence.
- Using your own level of clinical expertise.
- Considering patient values.

The politics of research

The government introduced the concept of 'Best Research for Best Health' (BRBH) in January 2006. The aim was to more directly improve patient benefit and research efficiency, with more direct links to public health, chronic disease and improved outcome. With this in mind the plan was to introduce increased funding to institutions providing high impact research, while 'automatic' funding to some institutions (for example some district general hospitals) would fall to zero. The pressure on teaching hospitals was to make solid plans to become successful research institutes, while district general hospitals had to make plans to collaborate with teaching institutions, or perhaps to attract industry money.

The immediate goals of BRBH were:

- Implementation: The amalgamation of National Institute for Healthcare Research (NIHR) and NICE together with the NHS Institute for Innovation and Improvement (NIII).
- Goal 1: NHS should be a Centre of Excellence.
- Goal 2: The United Kingdom should attract and retain the best research professionals through increased participation.
- Goal 3: Research should be focussed on improving health and social care.
- Goal 4: Knowledge resources should be managed properly, using formal guidelines, existing trials and improved access.
- Goal 5: Research institutes should be sound custodians of public money for public good.
- Additional Philosophy: There should be increased industry investment, decreased bureaucracy and increased utilisation of electronic data.

The NIHR was designed as a virtual body to coordinate research nationally. This contained within it a group of research networks, named UK Clinical Research Networks (UKCRN). These where 'topic specific' and local networks. The body also provided ethics and governance guidelines and support, in order to meet the goals of confidentiality together with the provision of legal and ethical guidelines. Plans were made for 'Academic Health Centres of the Future' (AHCF), institutions which would excel in research. The term 'translational research' was introduced to imply a direct relationship between the research bench to the bed side, and from the bed side to the community.

Research ethics committees are either local or multi-centre. Local research ethics committees (LREC) involve the relevant Health Authorities. Multi-centre research ethics committees (MREC) cover the whole of the United Kingdom for multi-centre trials. The Central Office for research ethics committees (COREC) provide administration for MRECs, management support for L-RECs and budget management. The National Patient Safety Agency: (NPSA) have responsibility for managing COREC.

The UKCRN is responsible for coordinating the topic specific networks and the local networks. The topic specific networks include:

- Cancer
- Children
- Dementia and Neuro-degenerative
- Diabetes
- Mental Health
- Stroke
- Primary Care.

The Comprehensive Local Research Network (CLRN) is a representation of both the NIHR and Higher Education Institutions. It supports higher education institutions, considers the interests and priorities of research projects, and reports to UKCRN. The CLRN employs a Clinical Director, who chairs the Board. The host site for the CLRN is normally a local teaching hospital; this institution organises human resources, finance, the premises and general facilities.

Questions you may be asked:

- What was your role in your research project?/What were the main conclusions?/ If you could repeat this research what would you change?

- Who funded/supported your research?/How was the funding achieved?

- Do you think all doctors should undertake research?

- Is research an area you wish to continue in? How will you achieve this?

- Can you account for why you have little research experience?

- How would you go about setting up a research project in a district general hospital?

- When finances are tight, how can you justify submitting a research project to the Trust which may need funding?

- How can you maximise funding for a research project in a district general hospital?

- Do you think EBM is effective?

- How can you maximise EBM?

Chapter 24 Key points:

Clinical audit

- Definition of Clinical Audit

- Pressures and advantages for performing Clinical Audit

- Participating Groups

- New guideline from an external credible source

- Types of triggers for Clinical Audit

- Implementation of findings (education)

- The stages involved in carrying out an audit

Research

- Definition

- Research governance

- Research implementation

- Evidence based medicine

- Politics of research.

Chapter 25 Continuing education and development

It is no longer considered acceptable for doctors to ignore the need to continue their education and development, even after achieving Consultant status. After the years of training, it is possible to feel, with genuine conviction, that you know 'enough' to do the job. However, hypotheses and intellectual viewpoints change, as does clinical evidence. The drive for clinical effectiveness is never-ending, and this may only be achieved with a good working knowledge of evidence-based medicine and an awareness of clinical controversies and issues. The Chief Medical Officer for England has emphasised the need for life-long learning to meet patients' needs and deliver NHS priorities. Therefore the government has identified this as a key responsibility of NHS Trusts; there is an earmarked budget designed to support this process. The whole medical infrastructure relies on doctors helping to train and teach their peers and junior colleagues. It is vital therefore that doctors show passion and enthusiasm for teaching. It is also important that all medical educators take a broad view about the topics that should be included in medical education. In addition to the accepted academic content, it may be essential to include the following topics in order to improve medical outcome:

- Management
- Corporate and political topics
- Healthcare ethics and the law

- Communication skills
- Information technology skills
- Skills in teaching, research, interviewing, and committee work.

Continuing Professional Development (CPD)

This is the means by which doctors improve and broaden their knowledge and skills and develop the personal qualities required in their professional lives. In addition it is a vehicle for doctors to take responsibility for their own ongoing development, the evidence of which will form the basis of appraisal (and eventually also validation, where the public can be assured that the doctor's education correlates with fitness to practice). It is a systematic and coherent approach to education. The medical Royal Colleges set standards for yearly CPD achievements and award educational courses time-based credits. Many strategies may be used to acquire CPDs; these may include reflective practice, audit, portfolio development and multi-disciplinary cooperation. The goal is the promotion of a culture in which doctors retain a curiosity about their subject that is a stimulant for lifelong learning.

Some characteristics of teaching include:

- Enthusiasm and passion
- Clear communication skills
- Sound knowledge base
- Ability to listen to and assess your students' learning progress
- Use of clear teaching materials
- Use of case studies to bring an applied approach to your teaching.

Problem-based learning (PBL)

This is an educational, academic concept of 'active learning' in tertiary education, especially within medicine. It was pioneered and used extensively at McMaster University, Hamilton, Ontario, Canada. Some defining characteristics of PBL are:

- Learning that is driven by challenging, open-ended problems.
- Students working in small collaborative groups.
- Teachers taking on the role as 'facilitators' of learning; students are encouraged to take responsibility for their group and to organise and direct the learning process with support from a tutor or instructor.
- A PBL cycle concludes with reflections on learning, problem solving, and collaboration.
- A structured system is used to help the learners keep track of their problem solving and learning.
- Feedback and reflection on the learning process and group dynamics are essential components of PBL.

Advocates of PBL claim it can be used to enhance content knowledge and foster the development of communication, problem-solving and self-directed learning skills.

Questions you might be asked regarding education:

- Why do you think continuing medical education is important?
- What is CPD?/What are the benefits of CPD?/How should CPD be regulated?
- How could you make education for your peers and junior staff more efficient?
- Talk us through your teaching experience.

- What makes you a good teacher?
- How do you assess competence for a given procedure in a colleague?
- What do you consider to be the most effective form of teaching?
- What is problem based learning? What are the advantages and disadvantages?

Chapter 25 Key points:

- The importance of continuing education

- CPD

- Some characteristics of good teaching

- PBL.

Chapter 26 Legal and ethical Issues

It is probable that legal and ethical issues impact daily on our medical lives. Topics include:

- Assessing the capacity of a patient
- Seeking consent
- The non-commencement or withholding of medical treatment
- End of life care
- Adverse incidents and medical error; implications for legal action and the sharing of information with patients and relatives
- Complaints; implications for legal action.

Assessing the capacity of a patient and the Mental Capacity Act (MCA)

The Mental Capacity Act 2005 has been fully in force since October 2007. This clarified the law with regard to dealing with the incapacitated patient, and codified the law with regard to best interests. It introduced the concept of substituted decision-making and placed advance refusals on a statutory footing. Lasting Powers of Attorney (LPA) were introduced as was the Independent Mental Capacity Advocate (IMCA). The aim was to introduce a code of practice to accompany legislation, and did not apply to treatment for mental disorders which would within the remit of the Mental Health Act.

The MCA suggests that there should be a presumption of capacity and re-enforces the philosophy that unwise decisions should not imply that the patient is incapable. Any acts performed on incapacitated patients must be in their best interests, and there should be an assessment as to whether a less restrictive option may achieve the clinical purpose.

The patient lacks capacity if he is unable to make a decision for himself because of impairment of, or disturbance in the functioning of, the mind or brain. This impairment may be permanent or temporary. The focus should be on the particular matter and the particular time when decision has to be made. The principle should be of equal consideration – the decision should not be based on age, appearance or unjustified assumptions.

The patient may be seen to be unable to make a decision if on balance of probabilities he is unable to:

- Understand the information relevant to the decision (as presented appropriately and with assistance.
- Retain that information (long enough to make a choice or decide.
- Use or weigh that information as part of the process of making the decision.
- Communicate his decision.

The person making the determination must consider all relevant circumstances and take the following steps (except in the case for advance refusals):

- Consider whether the patient will regain capacity in future.
- Involve the patient to the maximum extent possible.

- Consider (so far as reasonably ascertainable) past and present wishes and feelings of the patient, especially written wishes, and his relevant beliefs and values and other factors he would be likely to consider if able.
- If practicable and appropriate, consult and take into account views of anyone named by the patient; this may include non-family members who may be carers.
- Assess whether the act can be done in a less restrictive way.
- If issues concern life sustaining treatment, the determination should be in the patient's best interests, and not motivated by desire to bring about death.

The Act provides a defence to what would otherwise be assault for the patient possessing capacity, in connection with the clinical care or treatment of the patient. It should be clarified that reasonable steps have been taken to establish that the patient indeed does lack capacity, and the action must be in the patient's best interests. It should be noted that a valid and applicable advance refusal take precedence.

The determination of capacity should be within the remit of any clinician, however when there is sufficient doubt it may be reasonable to seek the help of a psychiatrist and the Trust legal team.

One example of an intervention is physical restraint of the patient. The latter is permissible only if necessary to prevent harm to the patient and this restraint should be proportionate to the likelihood and seriousness of harm. The restraint should be the most minimum that is required to achieve the desired outcome.

Lasting Powers of Attorney (LPA) extends to welfare (including healthcare) matters, in addition to property and financial matters. The individual creating the contract (and for whom the LPA is created) is termed the donor, and the individual who is given LPA status is termed the donee. This contract must be in a prescribed form, and registered to include the certificate of capacity from an independent person. The LPA donor may place restrictions on powers, and may provide for replacement. The donee may not appoint a successor, nor delegate authority. The donee is empowered to make healthcare decisions only once the donor is incapacitated. An advance refusal outranks the LPA unless the LPA is created after the advance refusal, and the LPA is valid and applicable. Life sustaining treatment may be provided when there is conflict with the LPA, pending a Court decision. Therefore in the event of disagreement between the doctor and the donee with regard to treatment, there is an obligation on the doctor to pursue the case to Court if necessary. If there is evidence of a possible failure by a donee to act in the best interests of the donor, this should lead to a reference to the Public Guardian. In situations where LPAs are seen to be invalid, there is protection given to donees and third parties relying on these LPAs.

Advance refusals must be valid and applicable. They will not be valid if:

- They are subsequently withdrawn.
- They are overridden by a subsequent applicable LPA.
- The patient has acted in a way which is clearly inconsistent with the decision.
- There were circumstances which existed which were not anticipated and these were likely to have affected the decision.

Advance refusals may be overridden in order to provide

treatment for a mental disorder of a patient detained formally under the Mental Health Act. It is for healthcare professionals to decide at first if the advance refusal is valid and applicable. If there are concerns, there is a duty of care to enquire to the Court of Protection. If the doctor reasonably believes that a valid and applicable advance refusal exists, there will be no liability if treatment is withheld. It is important however that if a doctor suspects that an advance refusal exists, reasonable efforts must be made, time permitting, to find out the detail; the doctor is permitted to act in the patient's best interests in an emergency.

Advance refusals only apply to refusals of treatment; patients may not make advance directives for specific treatments. It does not apply to life sustaining treatment unless it is stated in writing, and signed by or at the patient's direction and witnessed in writing.

Independent mental capacity advocates (IMCA) are instructed by an NHS body or local authority to represent and support an incapacitated patient before any decisions are made with regard to serious medical treatment, NHS arranged accommodation, a stay of 28 days or more in hospital, or a stay in a care home for eight weeks or more. This applies where no-one appropriate exists for the NHS body or local authority to consult with. The role of the IMCA is to advise on the patient's best interests, wishes, and to obtain further information. The IMCA is entitled to meet the patient in private and view the medical records. Information or submissions from the IMCA must be taken into account when providing care. The IMCA may challenge a decision; this is referred to the Court of Protection.

It is important to remember that the issues of capacity relate not only to day-to-day clinical scenarios, but also to the issue of consent to research.

Seeking a patient's consent

A good relationship between doctors and patients is built on trust. This is achieved by respecting the patients' autonomy, and their right to decide whether to undergo any medical intervention or not (even when their refusal may result in causing themselves harm or eventual death). This relates to the issues of capacity discussed above. When seeking their consent, patients must be provided with clear and sufficient information so that they can make an informed decision over their health care; effective communication is the key. The GMC suggests that the following points are addressed when seeking consent:

- Details of diagnosis and prognosis – and the likely prognosis if the condition is left untreated.
- Uncertainties about the diagnosis including options for further investigation prior to treatment.
- Options for treatment or management of the condition, including the option not to treat.
- Purpose of the proposed investigation or treatment.
- Details of the procedures or therapies involved, including:
  ○ Subsidiary treatment such as methods of pain relief.
  ○ How the patient should prepare for the procedure.
  ○ Details of what the patient might experience during or after the procedure including common and serious side effects.
- Explanations of the likely benefits and the probabilities of success.
- Discussion of any serious or frequently occurring risks, and of any lifestyle changes which may result from the treatment.

- Advice about whether a proposed treatment is experimental.
- How and when the patient's condition and any side effects will be monitored or re-assessed.
- The name of the doctor who will have overall responsibility for the treatment.
- Whether doctors undergoing training will be involved in delivering the treatment.
- Reminder that the patient can change their minds about a decision at any point in time.
- Reminder that the patient has the right to seek a second opinion.
- Where applicable a discussion of the costs involved.

Questions you may be asked:

- How often is the issue of capacity relevant in your specialty?
- Which experts would you involve to help you decide whether your patient has capacity?
- A typical scenario may be discussed involving withdrawal of or lack of consent for an intervention.

The non-commencement or withholding of medical treatment

Doctors have a responsibility to make the best interests of their patients their first concern. This is essential when considering any of the growing range of life-prolonging treatments which make it possible to extend the lives of patients who, through organ failure and life-threatening conditions, might otherwise die. The benefits of modern techniques such as cardiopulmonary resuscitation, renal dialysis, artificial ventilation, and artificial nutrition and hydration are considerable. However, any consideration for intervention has to be weighed against any perception that the natural end to life may be imminent (particularly with regard to chronic pathologies). The key word often is 'futility'. It is acceptable to withhold life-saving treatment if this same treatment is seen to be futile. However the definition of futility may be open to debate. Some would believe that in 'hopeless' cases with little or no hope of recovery, treatment may be withheld. Others would argue that the definition of 'hopeless' is open to debate, and treatment should only be withheld if the patient will definitely die despite the intervention. Often, reaching a satisfactory answer may mean addressing a number of difficult ethical and legal issues with the involvement of many different specialties and professions. The Trust legal team may have a role.

There may be some concerns in the public domain with regard to the possibility of over- or under-treatment towards the end of life. Some may feel that some doctors may make decisions about life-prolonging treatments without access to up to date clinical advice. It is also clear that the profession and patients want more guidance on what is considered ethically and legally permissible in this area. Patients and their families also want greater involvement in making these decisions with better arrangements to support them when facing these distressing situations.

It should be stressed that when it has been agreed that a certain intervention should not be commenced, the patient should receive full care and attention up to the point of the futile intervention. It is a common misconception for example that when patients are labelled 'not for cardiopulmonary resuscitation', that they are not for treatment. This misunderstanding may lead to confusion, errors, poor treatment and complaints.

End of life care

It may become obvious that the non-commencement or with-holding of medical treatment may lead to the dying process. Alternatively active treatment may be withdrawn (de-escalated) when futility is obvious. It is paramount in these situations that the patient (who is often unconscious and therefore lacks capacity) and their significant others are fully involved and aware, and are left in no doubt about the situation. Clarity and effective communication are essential skills in this context. In my experience when communication here is clear, the relatives though devastated, fully understand the situation. When there seems to be lack of understanding every effort should be made to improve communication; this may involve the introduction of other personnel. A common misconception, unfortunately promoted even by some healthcare professionals, is that the decision to withdraw treatment rests with the family of a dying patient. It is important to highlight that this decision is a clinical one and that the duty of the doctor is to explain the issues of futility articulately to the family.

However if despite all efforts the relatives of the dying patient disagree with the treatment de-escalation plans, the matter may sadly have to be referred to the courts. It is fortunate that this scenario is rare.

Terminal Care is defined as the care needed in the last few days of life. When this is embarked upon, high standards need to be adopted. The care may be best achieved when working collaboratively to facilitate a holistic approach:

- Staff need to recognise that the care of the dying patient is an important and integral part of the care offered to patients within the trust.

- Respect for patient autonomy, and informed decision-making in adults is promoted by honest and sensitive discussion with patients about care and treatment options. This includes helping those who wish to do so issue an advanced directive to inform future care at a time when they are no longer able to make decisions. Where this is not appropriate (e.g. confused or unconscious patients), discussion about care and treatment will occur with the family, taking into account previously known wishes and personal values of the patient.

- Staff need to recognise the need for patients to have choice and control over where death occurs. This includes acknowledgement that some patients want their terminal care provided in the hospital setting. Other patients may wish to have their terminal care at home or in the hospice setting.

- Visiting should be unrestricted for the terminal patient, and provision is made for relatives/carers to stay overnight with patients. Attention is paid to practical needs and concerns of patient, family, and friends.

- Staff should aim to ensure that patients wishes are respected in relation to who should be present at the time of death, recognising that different cultures may have different needs.

- Attention to pain relief, and other symptom control is recognised as a fundamental aspect of good terminal care.

- Psychological, social, and spiritual support for patients and families is a vital component of care throughout the dying process and in bereavement.

- All patients and staff should have access to the Trust's specialist Palliative Care Team if required.

- All patients and relatives should have access to the Trust's multi-faith Chaplaincy service and translation services if required.

- Patients must be afforded dignity and privacy. This is given irrespective of age, disability, gender, race, sexual orientation, spiritual beliefs, etc.
- Staff should receive support and education in order to offer an optimum service.

Questions you may be asked:
- Have you recently been involved in the de-escalation or withholding of treatment for any of your patients? What was your role? Who did you involve? What was the outcome?
- Are there circumstances in which withholding or withdrawing life-prolonging treatment would be unlawful?
- With regard to the withholding of treatment, what are the responsibilities in the decision-making process of the patient, doctor, healthcare team, family members and other people who are close to the patient? What weight should be given to their views?

Adverse incidents, medical error and complaints

The history, importance and philosophy of reporting adverse incidents and dealing with complaints have been dealt with in a previous chapter. Clearly there may be implications for legal action, and this will depend on the nature of the incident. The legal department of the Trust will normally take the lead in these cases, and will notify the relevant individuals. The responses in turn should be fed back to the Trust legal team, who then will be in a position to issue the Trust response.

It is also important to recognise that on discovery of an adverse incident, it may be relevant and prudent to inform the patient if there has been direct patient involvement; this should be done in a professional manner.

Questions you may be asked:

- Have you been involved in a legal case against the Trust? What was your role? How was the case resolved? Could the case have been handled better?

- Have you ever been charged with informing a patient about an adverse incident pertaining to his care?

- A scenario may be discussed where a patient needs to be informed about an adverse incident pertaining to his care.

Chapter 26 Key points:

- Assessing the capacity of a patient and the Mental Capacity Act (MCA)

- Seeking a patient's consent

- The non-commencement or withholding of medical treatment

- End of life care

- Adverse incidents, medical error and complaints, and implications for legal and ethical issues.

Chapter 27 Other key reports

Many important reports have been alluded to in previous chapters. The aim in identifying the additional reports below was to include those which had an impact on multiple and wide ranging topics

'Tooke' report: 'Aspiring to Excellence'.

This was the final report of the independent inquiry into Modernising Medical Careers, and was led by Professor Sir John Tooke. This was published in 2008.

The abstract of the report reads: 'MMC sought to reform postgraduate medical education and training to speed the production of competent specialists. Reform comprised: a two year foundation programme; centralised selection into "run-through" specialist training; the creation of fixed term specialist training appointments (FTSTAs); revisions to the non-consultant career grade. The Inquiry systematically analysed areas of concern arising from MMC: 1 Policy; 2 Professional engagement; 3 Workforce analysis; 4 Regulation; 5 Education and selection; 6 Training commissioning and management; 7 Service implications. The Panel proposed corrective action to resolve issues in the eight domains listed below. The resulting Interim Report with its associated recommendations was published on 8 October 2007. Consultation on the Report revealed strong agreement. 87 per cent of the 1,440 respondents agreed or strongly agreed with the 45 recommendations'.

The issues were as follows:

- The policy objective of postgraduate medical training was unclear. There was no consensus on the educational principles guiding postgraduate medical training. Moreover, there were no strong mechanisms for creating such consensus.

- There was no consensus on the role of doctors at various career stages.

- Weak DH policy development, implementation, and governance together with poor inter- and intra-Departmental links adversely affected the planned reform of postgraduate training.

- Medical workforce planning was hampered by lack of clarity regarding doctors' roles and did not align with other aspects of health policy. There was no structured policy regarding the potential massive increase in trainee numbers. Planning capacity was limited and training commissioning budgets were vulnerable in England, as they were held at SHA level.

- The medical profession's effective involvement in training policy-making had been weak.

- The management of postgraduate training was hampered by unclear principles, a weak contractual base, a lack of cohesion, a fragmented structure, and in England, deficient relationships with academia and service.

- The regulation of the continuum of medical education involved two bodies: GMC and PMETB, creating diseconomies in terms of both finance and expertise.

- The structure of postgraduate training proposed by MMC was unlikely to encourage or reward striving for excellence, offer appropriate flexibility to trainees, facilitate future workforce design, or meet the needs of particular groups (e.g.

those with academic aspirations, or those pursuing a non-consultant career grade experience). It risked creating another 'lost tribe' at FTSTA level.

Corrective action:

- There should be clear shared principles for postgraduate medical training that emphasise flexibility and an aspiration to excellence.
- Consensus on the role of doctors needed to be reached quickly, and the service contribution of trainees better acknowledged.
- DH policy development, implementation and governance should be strengthened. DH should appoint a lead for medical education, and strengthen collaboration.
- Workforce policy objectives should be integrated with training and service objectives. Medical workforce advisory machinery should be revised and enhanced. SHA workforce planning and commissioning should be subject to external scrutiny. Policies with respect to the current bulge in trainees and international medical graduates should be urgently resolved.
- The profession should develop a mechanism for providing coherent advice on matters affecting the entire profession.
- The accountability structure for postgraduate training and funding flows should be reviewed. Revised management structures should conform to agreed principles but reflect local circumstances. In England 'Graduate Schools' should be trialled where supported locally.
- PMETB should be merged within GMC to facilitate economies of scale, a common approach, linkage of accreditation

with registration and the sharing of quality enhancement expertise.

- The structure of postgraduate training should be modified to provide a broad based platform for subsequent higher specialist training, increased flexibility, the valuing of experience and the promotion of excellence.

Conclusion:

'To deal with many of the deficiencies identified and to ensure the necessary concerted action, the creation of a new body, NHS:Medical Education England (NHS:MEE) is proposed. NHS:MEE will relate to the revised medical workforce advisory machinery and act as the professional interface between policy development and implementation on matters relating to PGMET. It will promote national cohesion in England as well as working with equivalent bodies in the Devolved Administrations to facilitate UK wide collaboration. The Inquiry has charted a way forward and received a strong professional mandate. The recommendations and the aspiration to excellence they represent must not be lost in translation. NHS:MEE will help assure their implementation'.

The recommendations and conclusion of the report were accepted in principle, and plans for the merger of GMC and PMETB are already afoot, as described in a previous chapter.

Ara Darzi report

The main driver for this report was the perception that inequalities were rife in London, and that Londoners were not satisfied with health care. Lord Darzi (Sir Ara Darzi as he was then) set out a vision for change, and produced a document titled 'A Framework for Action'. The subject matter focussed on:

- The plans to tackle the predicted growth in population, particularly in the aged.
- Services focused on individual needs and choices.
- The philosophy of 'localise where possible, centralise where necessary', with regard to the provision of primary to tertiary health care.
- Truly integrated care and partnership working, maximising the contribution of the entire workforce.
- The philosophy that prevention is better than cure.
- A focus on health inequalities and diversity.
- A vision on models of health care, ranging from rehabilitation at home, through polyclinics to acute academic tertiary centres.

It is likely that many of the philosophies will apply to the evolution of health care in England within and outside London.

Kennedy report

From the late 1980s onwards, concerns about the performance of the Bristol Paediatric Cardiothoracic Unit were increasingly expressed in a variety of contexts. Some of these concerns were from healthcare professionals working in the Unit, while others were expressed by individuals in a variety of contexts outside the Unit. Rumours were common, and some appeared in the form of unattributed reports in the media. An operation performed on Joshua Loveday on 12 January 1995 proved to be the catalyst for further action. Joshua died on the operating table, and an external review was instituted. Complaints were subsequently made to the GMC concerning the conduct of two cardiac surgeons and of the Chief Executive of the Trust. They were found guilty in 1998 of serious professional misconduct. A group of parents of children who had undergone cardiac surgery at the BRI organised themselves to provide mutual support. In June 1996 the group first called for a Public Inquiry into the PCS services at the BRI.

The Kennedy report was published by the Bristol Royal Infirmary Inquiry in July 2001. The remit was:

- To inquire into the management of the care of children receiving complex cardiac surgical services at the Bristol Royal Infirmary between 1984 and 1995 and relevant related issues.
- To make findings as to the adequacy of the services provided.
- To establish what action was taken both within and outside the hospital to deal with concerns raised about the surgery.
- To identify any failure to take appropriate action promptly.
- To reach conclusions from these events.
- To make recommendations which could help to secure high-quality care across the NHS.

The Public Inquiry was conducted between October 1998 and July 2001. The Panel was chaired by Professor Ian Kennedy.

There were many recommendations. The significant ones included:

- The clinical process: patients should receive copies of any letters which are written about them; there was also the suggestion that patients should be offered the facility to make tape recordings of consultations.
- Informed consent: consent should be obtained for all examinations or procedures that involve any touching or physical contact with the patient.

- Working with other professional groups: the need for good clinical governance was demonstrated.

- Professional competence: the report revealed many failures of communication with patients and colleagues affecting all professional groups, and highlighted the need for instruction in communication skills for all healthcare professionals. The report, in emphasising the need for team work, recommended formal assessment of all aspects of competence including non-clinical elements of care, and placed continuing professional development (CPD) at the very centre of systems for assuring competence. Recommendations were also made for compulsory periodic appraisal for all health care professionals.

- Local teams and professional barriers: the report highlighted the increasing need for healthcare professionals to work in multi-disciplinary teams, and demonstrated many failures that arose from continued barriers between professional groups. Amongst the measures recommended by the report were the value of shared learning across professional boundaries, clinical audit, reflective practice, and leadership.

- Monitoring standards and performance: multi-disciplinary clinical audit was identified as a core vehicle for monitoring local performance.

- Adverse events and a 'no blame culture': recommendations were made that individual employees should be immune from disciplinary action when reporting adverse events.

- The external climate of the NHS: the report also served to highlight contributions to the Bristol tragedy made by under-funding and the concentration by governments on containing costs.

- Doctors and management: doctors engaged in management should be given sufficient time within their contracted hours to carry out those duties and they should receive specific training for the work.

It is clear that this report has relevance to many themes discussed elsewhere in this book.

Chapter 27 Key points:

- Tooke Report: Aspiring to Excellence. Training, education, roles.

- Darzi Report: growth in population, needs and choices, 'localise where possible, centralise where necessary', integrated care and partnership working, prevention is better than cure, health inequalities and diversity, models of health care.

- Kennedy Report: patient inclusion, informed consent, good clinical governance, professional competence, local teams and professional barriers, monitoring standards and performance, adverse events and a 'no blame culture', the external climate of the NHS, doctors and management.

Chapter 28 Questions of approach or 'scenario'

These questions test the candidate's methodology, wisdom, sharpness and decisiveness with regard to situations relating to key topics such as risk, complaints, fitness to practise, reputation (of the Department, the Trust, you and your colleagues), patient safety and welfare. As discussed in a previous chapter, one should rapidly identify the issue or problem; this may be followed by a demonstration of your methodology with a short introductory explanation, for example 'I believe this is a question of professional/criminal conduct' or 'I believe this is a question of ethics'.

The specialty

- Imagine that the Deanery has asked you as a new Consultant to entertain some new Foundation doctors; you have been given one hour to describe your specialty to them. What would you discuss?

The aim of this question is to summarise the specialty succinctly, and highlight the attraction.

- How would you dissuade a colleague from entering this specialty?

The disadvantages of the specialty are being sought. Clearly the candidate may wish to point out that in 'real life' there are several advantages which counterbalance the disadvantages.

• Imagine that you have been successful in this interview, and we have transported you ten years into the future. What do you see?

This question deals with ambition, both for the individual and the department/Trust.

Clinical risk

• Could you talk us through all the stages that an adverse incident form goes through:
  ◦ What would be the conclusion of a risk assessment for a needle stick injury?
  ◦ What would be the conclusion of a risk assessment for the booking and performance of an investigation (e.g. blood test or X-ray) on the wrong patient?

The description of the risk process is being sought. The second part of the question deals with the process of education and dissemination of information.

• Describe how you would deal with the situation if a few months into your new Consultant post, you are called to a cardiac arrest in Accident and Emergency. The arrest is over, and the patient is dead. Your team inform you that this man had suffered an out-of-hospital cardiac arrest, and was found to have a shockable cardiac rhythm on arrival in Accident and Emergency. The defibrillator did not work, and a substitute was sought. By the time the substitute defibrillator was available, the situation was no longer salvageable. The family are waiting in the relatives' room.

This question deals with: empathy (the dissemination of information to the family); knowledge of the risk process (identifying the problem in the machine and the checking process, removing the machine from clinical circulation, and pursuing the submission and follow-up of the risk form); time management (choosing the correct time to share information – it may be that the family require empathy there and then, while the machine incident may be discussed at a later date).

Complaints

- Describe how you would deal with the situation if four months into your new Consultant post, a patient verbally informs you of a grievance against:
  - A staff nurse on your ward.
  - A junior doctor on your firm.
  - A Consultant colleague in your specialty.

Awareness is needed of the procedures one may employ to: understand the patient; organise ways in which the issues may be dealt with, thereby minimising the chances of this grievance escalating.

- Describe how you would deal with the situation if four months into your new Consultant post, a patient hands you a written complaint, describing grievances against:
  - A Consultant colleague.
  - You and your team.

This deals with your knowledge of the written complaints process. The strategies employed in the verbal complaint above may also be used to resolve the situation.

Clinical effectiveness

- Describe what you would do if six months into your new Consultant post, you attend a very instructive clinical risk meeting which you feel would benefit patients through external scrutiny and openness.

The candidate is asked to describe the process of disseminating Trust information to the patients. The resources available should be described: directorate; clinical unit; operational manager; clinical director; Trust board; PALS; the local media. Knowledge should be demonstrated that it is likely that the Trust will delegate this duty to an executive officer and PALS. The philosophy is that the dissemination of information should be seen as a constructive act by all parties.

Doctors' performance

- Describe how you would deal with the situation if a few months into your new Consultant post, you discover:
  - A Consultant colleague who appears to be: arriving late for work; leaving early from work; taking longer to make clinical decisions; the subject of some coffee room conversations about these issues.
  - A Consultant colleague smelling of alcohol.
  - A Consultant colleague appearing to be drunk at work.
  - A Consultant colleague who is openly rude to patients and staff; this is noticed by patients.
  - A senior Consultant colleague watching child pornography on his laptop in the coffee room.
  - A junior doctor seemingly take a drug out of the drug cupboard, and put it in his mouth.

The under-performing doctor requires empathy and assistance while the doctor performing unprofessionally or criminally requires to go through due process. Patient safety is all important. Initially, it is vital that you confirm that any rumours or impressions are true, whether this applies to lateness, decision making or smelling of alcohol. If the individual has not been unprofessional, a private discussion may be all that is required. It should be made clear that you will personally take an interest in the doctor's performance and that you may have no option other than discussing this further with your senior colleagues if necessary. Hopefully the under-performing doctor will appreciate these discussions; if however he refuses to enter into a discussion with you, you may have to rapidly organise a formal meeting with your senior colleagues. If the issue with the doctor is a matter of fitness to practice (rudeness or criminal act), it is paramount that patients are protected. You should do your best to ensure that: you discuss your intended actions with the doctor; the doctor is removed from the clinical scene (if appropriate); patient care is maintained with alternative clinical cover; you discuss this with the Clinical Director, medical director and the legal team; you follow up the Trust response to this individual; you make further contributions to Trust decision making if you feel this is appropriate. It is also worth noting that many criminal acts (such as watching child pornography) require immediate correspondence with the police; this may be achieved by you or the Trust. It is also often appropriate that correspondence will be issued to the GMC on the grounds that there has been an issue of fitness to practice; this correspondence is often dealt with by the medical director.

- Describe how you would deal with the situation if a few months into your new Consultant post, you are offered:
  - Some money from a patient, in gratitude for your work.
  - A bottle of wine from a patient's relative, in gratitude for your work.
  - Some money for your department from a grateful patient.

This question deals with an awareness of professional

principles and probity. Money should never be accepted, unless a cheque is written to a nominated Trust charitable fund. Minor presents may be accepted at the discretion of the doctor. Gifts should be logged by all doctors, and letters of thanks should be issued by the Trust.

Ethics and law

- Describe how you would deal with the situation if a few months into your new Consultant post:
  - An elderly gentleman on your ward has repeatedly seemingly withdrawn his consent to an intervention which may be life-saving.
  - A patient has withdrawn his consent for an operation.

The issues of consent have been dealt with in detail in a previous chapter. Knowledge of the principles of consent and an awareness of the Trust resources (such as psychiatry and the legal team) need to be demonstrated.

- Describe how you would deal with the situation if a few months into your new Consultant post, your patient confidentially divulges his positive HIV status to you. He informs you that he is telling you this piece of information because he is worried that a new antibiotic drug that you have prescribed may react with some anti-retroviral drugs that he has been prescribed abroad. He does not want his GP, his wife or three other girlfriends to know his HIV status. He stresses that he simply requires reassurance with regard to the drug reactions.

This question deals with empathy and consent. It would be prudent to explain to the patient that it is unlikely that drugs will interact, if this is the primary concern. Professional skills should be used to the maximum in order to convince that patient that sharing this information with health professionals and social contacts will lead to better clinical care for him and those around him. It is important that other healthcare professionals, who may have some experience in this field, are also involved. If after discussions the patient will not change his mind, he should be told that the Trust will inform external professionals in order for them to provide the best clinical care for the social contacts. Legal advice should be sought at all times.

- Describe how you would deal with the situation if a few months into your new Consultant post, you feel that ongoing treatment for a particular patient is futile.
  - How would you initiate the decision making process?
  - Who would you involve in your discussions?
  - What are the responsibilities in the decision-making process of the patient, doctor, healthcare team, family members and other people who are close to the patient? What weight should be given to their views?

The de-escalation of treatment has been discussed elsewhere. The process should be multi-disciplinary and multi-specialty. The patient and relatives (the latter should be involved with the patient's consent, or in the event where the patient lacks capacity) should be intimately involved in discussions. There should be a clear distinction that relatives are not being burdened with the instruction to make a decision, but rather that views will be closely listened to.

- A few months into your new Consultant post, an adverse incident on your ward comes to light. A drug with a risk of causing bleeding has been prescribed to the wrong patient. The risk form has been submitted. Describe how you would arrange to inform the patient, and what you would say.

Time should be taken to speak to the patient in private. Empathy should be used, and the language should be simple to understand. Reassurance should be given (if appropriate) that no harm has occurred and that the clinical situation will be closely monitored. A description to the patient of the error would be important, together with any new processes which have been adopted for the prevention of a re-occurrence of this error. It is important that there should be a way for the patient to discuss any future queries with named healthcare professionals.

Chapter 28 Key points:

- Identify the topic being investigated

- Describe the process

- Patient safety is paramount

- Professional standards must be upheld.

Chapter 29 Ending the Interview

At the end of the interview you will almost certainly be asked: 'Do you wish to ask the panel anything?' It is vital that you do not undo all the good work that you have done. What you say at the end of your interview before you depart will leave a lasting impression on the members of the panel.

It may be appropriate to use questions as a vehicle to:

- Qualify or amplify a previous point
- Correct an earlier answer
- Clarify that you have no questions, as key personnel have dealt with your queries during your formal visit.

If you are appointed, there will be plenty of scope to have discussions with Medical Personnel in the time leading up to commencement of the job. It is therefore not appropriate to mention:

- Salaries
- Annual leave

It is perfectly acceptable to say 'I have no questions whatsoever'.

Ending the interview

When making your exit, you should make a point of acknowledging as many of the panel as possible. This may be manifested as a small nod and a 'thank you' addressed to the panel as a whole. When leaving, ensure you remember which door to exit from, if there is more than one. Walking into a broom cupboard will not leave the right kind of lasting impression.

Chapter 29 Key points:

- Choose your words carefully when you are asked: 'Have you any questions?'

- It is acceptable for you to say: 'I have no questions whatsoever'.

- Ending the interview: try to leave a lasting impression which is professional and courteous.

Chapter 30 Reports and other items for reference

Griffiths Report:
NHS Management Inquiry. Letter dated 6 October 1983 to the Secretary of State, Norman Fowler, from Roy Griffiths, Michael Betts, Jim Blyth and Sir Brian Bailey

The internal market:
Parliament. Working for patients. Cm 555. London: HMSO, 1989

The NHS Plan and precursors and sequelae:
The Health of the Nation. A strategy for health in England. July 1992. London HMSO. Cm1986
The new NHS – Modern, Dependable, 1997, London, HMSO, 1997 Cm 3807
The NHS Plan, A plan for investment, A plan for reform 2000, London HMSO
Securing our Future Health: Taking a Long-Term View, Final Report, Derek Wanless, April 2002, HM Treasury, London

Healthcare Commission:
http://www.healthcarecommission.org.uk/homepage.cfm

Adverse healthcare events and risk:
'An organisation with a memory': http://www.rcgp.org.uk/pdf/ISS_SUMM00_04.pdf
'Building a Safer NHS for Patients': http://www.dh.gov.uk/en/

Publicationsandstatistics/Publications/PublicationsPolicy
AndGuidance/Browsable/DH_4097460

NHS Direct:
http://www.nhsdirect.nhs.uk/

**Joint Guidance on Protecting Electronic Patient Information:
BMA/NHS Connecting for Health
National Service Frameworks**
http://www.dh.gov.uk/en/Healthcare/NationalServiceFrame
works/index.htm

Patient Advocacy and Liaison Service (PALS):
http://www.dh.gov.uk/en/Managingyourorganisation/
PatientAndPublicInvolvement/Patientadviceandliaison
services/index.htm

NICE:
http://www.nice.org.uk/

Healthcare resource groups and 'Payment by Results':
http://www.ic.nhs.uk/casemix

MMC:
http://www.mmc.nhs.uk/

HAN:
http://www.healthcareworkforce.nhs.uk/hospitalatnight.html

Clinical Governance:
http://www.dh.gov.uk/en/Publichealth/Patientsafety/Clinical
governance/index.htm

Clinical audit:
http://www.cgsupport.nhs.uk/Resources/Clinical_Audit/
1@Introduction_and_Contents.asp

Research:
Best Research for Best Health, A new national health research strategy, Department of Health

Mental Capacity Act:
Mental Capacity Act 2005 – summary, Department of Constitutional affairs, Department of Health, Public Guardianship Office, Welsh Assembly Government

The Royal Liverpool Children's Inquiry. Summary and Recommendation. Ordered by The House of Commons to be printed January 30 2001

The Human Tissue Act 2004. New legislation on human organs and tissue. Department of Health

Tooke report:
Final report of the Independent Inquiry into Modernising Medical Careers led by Professor Sir John Tooke

Medical Leadership Competency Framework:
Enhancing Engagement in Medical Leadership Project Draft. April 2008. Academy of Medical Royal Colleges. Institute for Innovation and Improvement.

Darzi report:
A Framework for action, Professor Sir Ara Darzi

Kennedy report:
http://www.bristol-inquiry.org.uk/final_report/Summary.pdf

New for 2009

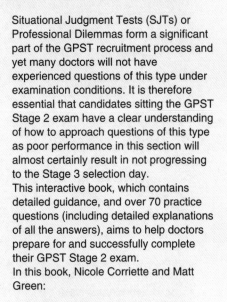
Situational Judgment Tests (SJTs) or Professional Dilemmas form a significant part of the GPST recruitment process and yet many doctors will not have experienced questions of this type under examination conditions. It is therefore essential that candidates sitting the GPST Stage 2 exam have a clear understanding of how to approach questions of this type as poor performance in this section will almost certainly result in not progressing to the Stage 3 selection day.

This interactive book, which contains detailed guidance, and over 70 practice questions (including detailed explanations of all the answers), aims to help doctors prepare for and successfully complete their GPST Stage 2 exam.

In this book, Nicole Corriette and Matt Green:

- Describe the context of Situational Judgement Tests within the GPST Stage 2 selection process
- Explore the various ethical principles that you must consider when answering these types of questions
- Set out how to approach the various question types you will be faced with
- Provide over 70 questions to put into practise everything that you learn
- Detailed explanations of the correct answers are also provided to aid your preparations

This engaging, easy to use and comprehensive book is essential reading for anyone serious about excelling in their GPST Stage 2 examination and successfully progressing to Stage 3 of the GPST selection process.

For more information visit

www.Apply2Medicine.co.uk

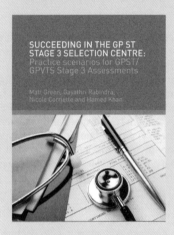